MEDITERRANEAN DIET COOKBOOK FOR SENIORS

Super Easy 15-Minute Recipes to Support Weight Loss, Heart Health and Vitality

Grace Moretti

© COPYRIGHT 2024 - ALL RIGHTS RESERVED.

No part of this publication may be reproduced, stored in a retrieval system, or transmitted in any form or by any means—electronic, mechanical, photocopying, recording, or otherwise—without the prior written permission of the author or publisher, except for brief quotations used in reviews or scholarly works.

This book is intended for personal, non-commercial use only. You may not edit, distribute, sell, or reuse any part of this content without written permission from the author or publisher.

Disclaimer

This cookbook is for informational and educational purposes only and is not intended as a substitute for professional medical advice, diagnosis, or treatment. Always consult your physician or a qualified healthcare provider before making any changes to your diet, especially if you have any pre-existing medical conditions or dietary restrictions.

The author and publisher have made every effort to ensure the information provided is accurate and up to date at the time of publication. However, nutritional science evolves, and individual needs vary. The author and publisher disclaim any liability for any loss, injury, or damage incurred as a result of the use or misuse of the information presented in this book.

By reading this book, you acknowledge that the author and publisher are not responsible for any outcomes that may arise from following the recipes, suggestions, or guidance provided.

CONTENTS

INTRODUCTION	09
CHAPTER 1: BENEFITS OF THE MEDITERRANEAN DIET	10
The Core Principles of the Mediterranean Diet	12
Key Benefits for Heart Health and Longevity	16
Impact on Weight Management and Vitality	18
It's More Than Just Food	21
CHAPTER 2: COOKING ESSENTIALS FOR SENIORS	22
Practical Kitchen Tools and Time-Saving Strategies	23
Essential Mediterranean Ingredients for Flavor and Nutrition	25
Simplicity is the Answer	27
CHAPTER 3: BREAKFAST	29
Savory Avocado Toast with Cherry Tomatoes & Olive Oil	30
Greek Yogurt with Honey, Walnuts & Fresh Berries	31
Spinach & Feta Egg Scramble	32
Mediterranean Oats with Almonds, Dates & Cinnamon	33
Tomato, Basil & Mozzarella Breakfast Sandwich	34
Cucumber, Hummus & Smoked Salmon Wrap	35
Chickpea Breakfast Hash with Bell Peppers & Onions	36
Ricotta & Fig Toast with Walnuts	37
Mediterranean Smoothie with Spinach, Banana & Olive Oil	38
Poached Eggs with Sauteed Kale & Garlic	39
Warm Quinoa Breakfast Bowl with Almond Milk & Berries	40
Zucchini & Herb Omelette with Goat Cheese	41
Apple-Cinnamon Chia Pudding (Prepped the Night Before)	42
Whole Grain Pita with Hummus, Sliced Egg & Cucumber	43
Red Pepper & Goat Cheese Breakfast Wrap	44
Mediterranean Cottage Cheese Bowl	45
Almond Butter & Banana Toast with Chia Seeds	46
Herbed Tomato & Egg Skillet	47
Apricot & Walnut Greek Yogurt Bowl	48

CHAPTER 4: LUNCH — 49

- Grilled Chicken Shawarma Bowl 50
- Mediterranean Lentil Salad 51
- Tuna & White Bean Salad 52
- Stuffed Bell Peppers with Quinoa & Feta 53
- Baked Falafel Lettuce Wraps 54
- Zucchini Noodles with Pesto & Cherry Tomatoes 55
- Grilled Eggplant & Chickpea Wrap 56
- Salmon & Farro Grain Bowl 57
- Mediterranean Turkey Burger 58
- Greek Chickpea Stew 59
- Caprese Quinoa Bowl 60
- Herbed Chicken Pita Pocket 61
- Shrimp & Orzo Salad 62
- Vegetable & Feta Stuffed Pita 63
- Mediterranean Tuna-Stuffed Avocados 64
- Chickpea & Spinach Patties 65
- Roasted Cauliflower & Lentil Bowl 66
- Eggplant & Tomato Stew (Caponata Style) 67
- Sardine & Avocado Toast 68
- Lentil & Feta-Stuffed Sweet Potatoes 69
- Chicken Souvlaki Skewers with Tzatziki 70
- Spinach & Olive Whole Grain Pasta 71
- Bulgur Salad with Parsley & Pomegranate 72
- Roasted Red Pepper & Hummus Wrap 73
- Baked Cod with Tomato & Olive Tapenade 74

CHAPTER 5: DINNER — 75

- Lemon Herb Baked Chicken Thighs 76
- Baked Eggplant Parmesan (Lightened Up) 77
- Grilled Sea Bass with Olive Tapenade 78
- One-Pan Mediterranean Chicken & Veggies 79
- Chickpea & Spinach Curry with Brown Rice 80
- Stuffed Zucchini Boats with Turkey & Feta 81
- Salmon with Lemon-Dill Yogurt Sauce 82
- Vegetarian Moussaka 83
- Greek Lemon Chicken Soup (Avgolemono) 84
- Shrimp Saganaki with Tomatoes & Feta 85
- Grilled Lamb Chops with Rosemary & Garlic 86
- Stuffed Bell Peppers with Rice & Herbs 87

Baked Tilapia with Herbed Quinoa 88
Lentil & Sweet Potato Stew 89
Cauliflower & Chickpea Tagine 90
Spinach & Feta Stuffed Chicken Breast 91
Mediterranean Vegetable Casserole 92
Seared Tuna with White Bean Salad 93
Quinoa-Stuffed Tomatoes with Basil & Goat Cheese 94
Roasted Chicken Drumsticks with Garlic & Paprika 95
Eggplant & Lentil Ragu over Whole Wheat Pasta 96
Zucchini Noodle Stir-Fry with Tofu 97
White Fish en Papillote with Lemon & Herbs 98
Stuffed Portobello Mushrooms with Couscous 99
Chard & Cannellini Bean Sauté 100

CHAPTER 6: DESSERTS   101

Greek Yogurt with Honey & Walnuts 102
Olive Oil Citrus Cake (Naturally Sweetened) 103
Fig & Almond Energy Bites 104
Lemon Yogurt Mousse with Olive Oil 105
Baked Pears with Cinnamon & Walnuts 106
Tahini Bliss Balls with Dates & Sesame Seeds 107
Orange & Almond Flour Cookies 108
Ricotta with Berries & Balsamic Glaze 109
Spiced Poached Apples in Herbal Tea 110
Coconut Date Rolls 111
Mini Greek Yogurt Cheesecakes (No-Bake) 112
Rosewater Pistachio Bites 113
Chia Pudding with Almond Milk & Figs 114
Baked Medjool Dates Stuffed with Almond Butter 115
Spiced Fig Compote with Greek Yogurt 116
Sesame-Honey Bars (Pasteli) 117
Apricot & Almond Couscous Pudding 118

CHAPTER 7: EVERYDAY SNACKS   119

Hummus with Veggie Sticks 120
Stuffed Grape Leaves (Dolmas) 121
Cucumber & Feta Bites 122
Mini Caprese Skewers 123
Marinated Olives with Orange Zest 124
Roasted Red Pepper Hummus 125

Whole Grain Pita with Tzatziki 126
Spiced Roasted Chickpeas 127
Greek Yogurt & Herb Dip with Crackers 128
Baba Ghanoush with Seed Crackers 129
Mini Falafel Balls with Tahini Sauce 130
Tomato Bruschetta on Whole Grain Toast 131
Zucchini Fritters with Yogurt Dip 132
Hard-Boiled Eggs with Olive Tapenade 133
Lentil & Herb Salad Cups 134
Ricotta-Stuffed Cherry Tomatoes 135
Mini Spinach & Feta Phyllo Triangles 136
Smoked Salmon on Cucumber Rounds 137
Warm Herbed Olives & Almonds 138
Mini Bell Peppers Stuffed with Hummus 139

CHAPTER 8: SMOOTHIES, TEAS & JUICES — 140

Spinach, Banana & Olive Oil Smoothie 141
Fig & Almond Smoothie 142
Greek Yogurt & Berry Smoothie 143
Avocado-Cucumber Mint Smoothie 144
Orange-Date Smoothie with Tahini 145
Zucchini & Pineapple Smoothie 146
Cherry-Pomegranate Smoothie 147
Watermelon-Basil Smoothie 148
Pear & Ginger Smoothie 149
Coconut-Yogurt Smoothie with Pistachios 150
Chamomile & Lemon Balm Tea 151
Mint & Green Tea Infusion 152
Sage & Rosemary Herbal Tea 153
Fennel & Licorice Root Tea 154
Olive Leaf Tea with Lemon 155
Carrot, Orange & Ginger Juice 156
Cucumber-Lemon Detox Water 157
Pomegranate-Mint Cooler 158
Celery, Apple & Parsley Juice 159
Warm Lemon Water with Olive Oil 160

BONUS: 28-DAY MEAL PLAN — 161
A FINAL TOAST TO MEDITERRANEAN LIVING — 166
REFERENCES — 168

INTRODUCTION

When I first started pursuing my nutrition degree in college, I faced an ironic problem—I began gaining weight. It was embarrassing, especially since I was pursuing a career in health and wellness. But then it hit me: the stress of school, combined with endless takeout meals, was draining my energy and adding pounds. What I truly missed were my mother's homemade Mediterranean dishes—the vibrant flavors, the wholesome ingredients, the way they made me feel nourished and energized. That's when I realized: the key to feeling my best wasn't in complicated diet trends, but in returning to the simple, delicious foods I grew up with.

What if eating well could be both delicious and life-changing? That's the heart of the Mediterranean diet—a way of eating that's as joyful as it is nourishing. Inspired by the traditions of Southern Europe and the long-lived communities of the "Blue Zones," this diet isn't just about food—it's about savoring meals that boost heart health, energy, and longevity.

As we age, staying healthy means staying independent. The Mediterranean diet makes that simple. Think fresh vegetables, whole grains, olive oil, and lean proteins—meals that are as vibrant and satisfying as they are good for you. Picture starting your day with creamy Greek yogurt and honey, enjoying a crisp Greek salad for lunch, or savoring herb-roasted fish for dinner. Every bite is a step toward better health, without deprivation or dull flavors.

We know that cooking can feel overwhelming at times, so we've made it easy. Inside, you'll find quick, flavorful recipes that fit into your life—no complicated steps or hours in the kitchen. Whether it's a 15-minute meal or a dish to share with loved ones, these recipes prove that eating well can be effortless and delicious.

The Mediterranean diet isn't a short-term fix—it's a lasting way to enjoy food, health, and life at any age. Let this book guide you toward meals that nourish your body and lift your spirit. Here's to good food, good health, and many more joyful moments around the table. Welcome to the Mediterranean way of life.

CHAPTER 1: BENEFITS OF THE MEDITERRANEAN DIET

CHAPTER 1: BENEFITS OF THE MEDITERRANEAN DIET

Sophia, a retiree in a sun-drenched Sicilian village, still smiles when she remembers the lively gatherings of years past. Every evening, her family and neighbors would crowd around a weathered wooden table, passing plates of ruby-red tomatoes drizzled with golden olive oil, crusty bread still warm from the oven, and creamy wedges of local cheese. The air buzzed with laughter, the clink of glasses, and the easy rhythm of shared stories.

But lately, something had shifted. Though her days were still filled with good food and good company, Sophia couldn't ignore the heavy fatigue that lingered after meals or the way her clothes had begun to fit a little tighter. "How can this be?" she'd wonder, stirring a pot of simmering vegetables. "I eat the way I always have." Yet the energy that once came so naturally now felt just out of reach.

Like many of us, Sophia had unknowingly drifted from the true heart of the Mediterranean way of life—not just its ingredients, but its rhythms. The long walks to the market, the afternoon rests, the mindful enjoyment of each bite. In this chapter, we'll explore how returning to these simple, nourishing habits can reignite vitality, protect the heart, and add years to life—not through restriction, but through joy. Sophia's story, and perhaps yours, isn't about giving up the foods she loves, but rediscovering how to savor them in a way that loves her back.

Because the secret wasn't just on her plate. It was in the pace of her day, the company she kept, and the permission to relish every sun-soaked moment. Let's uncover how you can bring that same wisdom—and that same lightness—back to your own table.

The Core Principles of the Mediterranean Diet

This isn't just a diet—it's a 2,000-year-old love story between people and their food. The Mediterranean diet's magic lies in its beautiful simplicity: fresh ingredients prepared with care, shared with joy.

What makes it truly special? Ten timeless principles passed down through generations of fishermen, farmers, and grandmothers who knew the secret to both good food and good living. These aren't restrictive rules, but rather an invitation to:

- Savor nature's bounty at its seasonal peak
- Let vegetables take center stage
- Make every meal a celebration of flavor and connection

From the first press of olive oil to the last sip of evening wine, each element works together to nourish both body and soul. As you'll discover in these pages, this is eating the way nature intended - vibrant, varied, and deeply satisfying.

Now, let's explore these life-giving principles that have kept Mediterranean communities healthy and happy for centuries.

1. Olive Oil: Your Daily Dose of Liquid Sunshine

Every Mediterranean kitchen has one constant—a bottle of extra virgin olive oil (EVOO) front and center. Unlike processed oils, EVOO is packed with heart-healthy monounsaturated fats and polyphenols that fight inflammation (Capurso, 2024).

How to use it daily:

- Drizzle over salads, soups, and grilled fish
- Use for low-heat cooking (it smokes at high temps)
- Dip whole-grain bread in EVOO with balsamic vinegar

2. Eat the Seasons—Like a Mediterranean Grandmother

Before supermarkets, people ate what grew nearby. Seasonal food is fresher, more nutritious, and often cheaper (ALTOMARE et al., 2013).

Seasonal eating made easy:

- **Spring:** Artichokes, asparagus, strawberries
- **Summer:** Tomatoes, zucchini, peaches
- **Fall:** Figs, mushrooms, pomegranates
- **Winter:** Citrus, kale, root vegetables

Pro tip: Frozen fruits/veggies count! Stock up when seasonal produce is cheap.

3. The Joy of Shared Meals

In Greece, they say "we don't eat to live—we live to eat." Shared meals reduce stress and improve digestion by slowing you down (Capurso, 2024).

How to bring this home:

- Make Sunday dinners device-free
- Host potlucks where everyone brings a dish
- Eat outdoors when possible—even picnics count!

4. Plants Take Center Stage

Vegetables aren't side dishes—they're the star. Try filling half your plate with colorful produce at every meal (Altomare et al., 2013).

Simple ways to eat more plants:

- Start meals with a vegetable soup or salad
- Blend spinach into smoothies
- Snack on raw veggies with hummus

5. Seafood Twice a Week

Fatty fish like salmon and sardines are rich in omega-3s that boost brain health and fight inflammation (Capurso, 2024).

Budget-friendly seafood ideas:

- Canned tuna in olive oil
- Frozen shrimp
- Mussels (often cheaper than other shellfish)

6. Whole Grains for Sustained Energy

Swap refined grains for nutrient-packed whole grains like farro, bulgur, and whole-wheat pasta (Altomare et al., 2013).

Easy swaps:

- Choose brown rice instead of white
- Try whole-wheat couscous
- Use whole-grain bread for toast

7. Herbs & Spices: Nature's Medicine Cabinet

Mediterranean cooking uses herbs and spices instead of salt for flavor—many have health benefits too (Capurso, 2024).

Must-have herbs/spices:

- Garlic (lowers cholesterol)
- Oregano (antibacterial properties)
- Turmeric (anti-inflammatory)

8. Tomatoes: A Superfood in Disguise

Cooked tomatoes provide lycopene, which may reduce cancer risk (Altomare et al., 2013).

Ways to enjoy:

- Homemade marinara sauce
- Slow-roasted cherry tomatoes
- Sun-dried tomatoes in salads

9. Dairy: Quality Over Quantity

Fermented dairy like Greek yogurt and feta cheese offer probiotics and calcium without excess saturated fat (Capurso, 2024).

Smart choices:

- Plain Greek yogurt with honey and nuts
- Small portions of aged cheeses
- Kefir as a probiotic drink

10. Wine: If You Drink, Do It Mediterranean-Style

Red wine in moderation (1 glass/day for women, 2 for men) may benefit heart health (Altomare et al., 2013).

Alternatives:

- Pomegranate juice
- Herbal teas
- Sparkling water with citrus

The Mediterranean diet isn't about perfection—it's about enjoying real food with people you love. Start small by adding more vegetables to your plate or switching to olive oil. Your body, mind and taste buds will thank you!

Key Benefits for Heart Health and Longevity

For older adults, the Mediterranean diet offers more than just good nutrition—it's a delicious path to protecting your heart, sharpening your mind, and maintaining your independence. Science shows this way of eating can help you feel better today while adding healthier years to your life.

Proven Heart Protection

Clinical studies reveal the Mediterranean diet helps seniors by:

- ✓ Lowering bad cholesterol while maintaining good cholesterol (Ros et al., 2014)
- ✓ Reducing blood pressure and artery inflammation (Widmer et al., 2015)
- ✓ Cutting risk of heart disease by nearly one-third

The Longevity Advantage

In Mediterranean regions where people regularly live active lives into their 90s, their plates typically feature:

- ✓ Colorful fruits and vegetables packed with age-defying antioxidants
- ✓ Omega-3 rich fish that nourishes both heart and brain
- ✓ Whole grains that provide steady energy without sugar crashes

Senior-Friendly Benefits

This diet adapts perfectly to aging bodies:

- ✓ Cooked vegetables and legumes are easy to digest
- ✓ Healthy fats help your body absorb nutrients better
- ✓ Flexible portions accommodate changing appetites
- ✓ Shared meals combat loneliness and stress (Ros et al., 2014)

Mediterranean Foods for Common Aging Concerns

Concern	Mediterranean Solutions	Easy Prep Tips
Arthritis	Fatty fish (salmon, sardines), olive oil, nuts	Try canned salmon on whole-grain toast
Memory Support	Walnuts, berries, leafy greens, olive oil	Blend spinach into morning smoothies
Bone Health	Greek yogurt, cheese, sardines with bones	Make yogurt parfaits with layers of fruit
Digestive Health	Lentils, chickpeas, cooked vegetables	Simmer lentils into soft, flavorful soups
Low Energy	Whole grains, bananas, nuts, olive oil	Keep trail mix with nuts and dried fruit handy

Adapting for Chewing or Dental Challenges

- ✓ Choose soft-cooked vegetables over raw
- ✓ Opt for flaky fish instead of tough meats
- ✓ Blend soups with beans and olive oil
- ✓ Mash avocado on whole-grain bread
- ✓ Soak whole-grain bread in olive oil and tomato sauce

Simple Changes, Big Results

Start with these easy switches:

- ✓ Replace butter with olive oil
- ✓ Enjoy fish twice weekly (canned options work great)
- ✓ Choose nuts over processed snacks
- ✓ End meals with fresh fruit instead of sugary desserts

Research confirms this enjoyable, sustainable approach offers some of the best protection for your heart and longevity (Widmer et al., 2015). The best part? Every flavorful meal brings you both pleasure and health benefits.

Impact on Weight Management and Vitality

The Mediterranean diet represents a paradigm shift in our understanding of healthy weight management, particularly for older adults. Unlike conventional weight loss approaches that focus primarily on calorie restriction, this dietary pattern offers a holistic solution that nourishes the body while naturally regulating weight. Its effectiveness stems from centuries of culinary tradition refined by modern nutritional science, creating a sustainable approach to maintaining vitality throughout the aging process.

Sustainable Weight Management

The Mediterranean diet's effectiveness for weight regulation lies in its synergistic combination of nutrient-dense foods and eating behaviors. The high fiber content from its emphasis on whole plant foods operates on multiple levels to support healthy weight. Soluble fiber forms a gel-like substance in the digestive tract that slows gastric emptying, prolonging feelings of fullness (Kim, 2020). Insoluble fiber adds bulk to meals without significant calories, allowing for satisfying portion sizes. This fiber matrix also modulates gut microbiota composition, with emerging research suggesting certain bacterial strains may influence metabolic efficiency and fat storage.

The diet's inclusive nature addresses a critical flaw in restrictive diets—psychological deprivation. By permitting moderate amounts of traditionally forbidden foods like whole grain breads and quality cheeses, it prevents the binge-restrict cycle that sabotages long-term weight management. This psychological sustainability is further enhanced by:

- Cultural celebration of food as pleasure rather than mere fuel
- Flexible framework adaptable to personal tastes and traditions
- Social reinforcement through shared meal experiences

Natural Energy Enhancement

The Mediterranean diet's macronutrient profile is uniquely suited to support the changing energy needs of older adults. Its complex carbohydrates provide a steady glucose release due to their low glycemic index, preventing the blood sugar spikes and crashes associated with refined grains (Doctor's Desk, 2023). This stable energy supply is particularly valuable for maintaining cognitive function and physical endurance throughout the day.

The diet's emphasis on monounsaturated and omega-3 fatty acids offers several energy-related benefits:

- Enhanced mitochondrial function in aging cells
- Improved neurotransmitter synthesis for brain health
- Reduced systemic inflammation that can cause fatigue
- Better absorption of fat-soluble vitamins that support metabolism

Protein sources in the Mediterranean diet are carefully balanced to preserve lean muscle mass while avoiding the renal stress of high-protein diets. The combination of plant proteins from legumes with marine and dairy proteins provides a complete amino acid profile optimized for aging physiology.

Practical Adaptations for Older Adults

Implementing the Mediterranean diet requires thoughtful adaptation to address common age-related challenges. For those with dental concerns or decreased saliva production:

- Softer preparations like roasted vegetables retain more nutrients than boiling
- Finely chopped nuts can replace whole nuts for easier chewing
- Hummus and other bean spreads offer plant protein in creamy forms

For individuals managing multiple medications:

- High-vitamin K foods can be balanced for those on blood thinners
- Grapefruit limitations can be addressed with alternative citrus
- Fiber increases should be gradual to prevent medication absorption issues

Cognitive considerations include:

- Simple, repetitive meal structures to reduce decision fatigue
- Visually appealing plate arrangements to stimulate appetite
- Familiar flavors with nutrient-dense upgrades

Documented Benefits

Longitudinal studies of Mediterranean diet adherence demonstrate compelling outcomes for older populations (Doctor's Desk, 2023):

- 23% lower risk of frailty over 4 years
- Significant preservation of muscle mass
- Better maintenance of resting metabolic rate
- Improved physical performance scores

The diet's anti-inflammatory effects appear particularly valuable for mitigating age-related sarcopenia and supporting joint health. Its positive impact on gut microbiota diversity may explain some of these protective effects against frailty.

A Day of Nourishment

A closer examination of sample meals reveals the nutritional sophistication of this approach:

Breakfast: Greek yogurt provides probiotics for gut health, while walnuts contribute alpha-linolenic acid and melatonin precursors that support circadian rhythms in older adults.

Lunch: Lentil soup delivers approximately 18g of plant protein per serving along with resistant starch that feeds beneficial gut bacteria. The accompanying whole grain bread offers B vitamins often deficient in aging populations.

Dinner: Fatty fish like salmon provides the EPA and DHA forms of omega-3s that are most bioavailable for brain and heart health. The roasted vegetables supply antioxidants that become more concentrated through the caramelization process.

Implementation Stratgies

For successful adoption, consider:

1. A phased approach beginning with easily achievable changes like switching cooking oils
2. "Mediterraneanizing" familiar dishes rather than complete overhauls
3. Building a supportive food environment through pantry stocking
4. Social reinforcement through cooking classes or meal sharing

The Mediterranean diet's true power lies in its ability to transform weight management from a stressful obligation into a natural outcome of joyful, nourishing eating. By addressing the biological, psychological, and social aspects of nutrition, it offers older adults a path to sustained vitality that honors both science and tradition.

It's More Than Just Food

The Mediterranean diet transcends nutrition—it's a celebration of life's later chapters. By embracing its whole-food philosophy and communal spirit, seniors gain more than health benefits; they rediscover the joy of eating. This approach naturally supports heart health, stable energy, and comfortable weight management through simple, flavorful choices.

Its true power lies in adaptability—whether modifying textures, simplifying meals, or preserving cherished food traditions. Each olive oil-dressed vegetable, each fish supper shared with loved ones, becomes an investment in vitality.

This isn't about restriction, but about savoring quality years. The Mediterranean way proves that aging well can be delicious, social, and deeply satisfying—one mindful meal at a time.

CHAPTER 2: COOKING ESSENTIALS FOR SENIORS

CHAPTER 2: COOKING ESSENTIALS FOR SENIORS

The kitchen has always been more than just a place to prepare meals—it's where memories are made, recipes tell stories, and love is shared through food. But as we age, familiar kitchen tasks can become unexpectedly challenging.

Consider Anne, a retired teacher who once took pride in her from-scratch cooking. These days, her favorite knife feels awkward in her hands, and standing at the counter leaves her fatigued. Like many seniors, she finds herself torn between her passion for cooking and the physical realities of aging.

This chapter offers practical solutions to keep the joy of cooking alive. We'll explore senior-friendly tools, time-saving techniques, and smart kitchen adaptations that transform meal prep from a chore back into the pleasure it should be—because everyone deserves to cook with comfort, confidence, and joy.

Practical Kitchen Tools and Time-Saving Strategies

Cooking should remain a joyful and fulfilling activity at any age. For seniors, having the right tools and techniques can make all the difference.

Essential Ergonomic Tools Checklist

- Easy-grip knives with angled blades (require 30% less force than standard knives) (*Simplify Meal Prep*, 2024)
- Non-slip cutting boards with suction feet or silicone edges
- Lightweight cookware (under 3 lbs for pots/pans)
- Large-button electric appliances (food processors, can openers)
- Adjustable jar opener with rubberized grip
- Ergonomic measuring cups with bold, high-contrast markings

Kitchen Organization Guide

Visual layout for an accessible workspace:

- **Primary Zone:** Keep daily-use items (utensils, oils, spices) within arm's reach (15-20" from counter edge)
- **Secondary Zone:** Store weekly-use appliances (blender, mixer) on wheeled cart
- **Auxiliary Zone:** Place seasonal/specialty items in labeled upper cabinets

Pro tip: Use lazy susans in corner cabinets to maximize accessibility.

Batch Cooking Time Reference

- Lentil Soup: 15 min prep, 45 min cook, freezes well (3 months)
- Ratatouille: 20 min prep, 1 hour cook, freezes well (2 months)
- Whole Grains: 5 min prep, 30-50 min cook, freezes well (6 months)

Time-Saving Techniques

- The Two-Tool Principle: Design meals requiring no more than two main tools (knife + pot)
- Pre-Cut Advantage: Nutritionally equivalent frozen vegetables save prep time (*Elder-Friendly Kitchen Essentials*, 2024)
- Layered Cooking: Use oven-safe pots to cook grains and vegetables simultaneously

Technology Enhancements

- Voice-controlled timers for hands-free monitoring
- Recipe organization apps with senior-friendly interfaces
- Shared digital grocery lists for family coordination

Essential Mediterranean Ingredients for Flavor and Nutrition

Building on our exploration of kitchen tools and techniques, we now turn to the heart of Mediterranean cooking: wholesome, flavorful ingredients that nourish both body and soul. For seniors, these culinary staples offer more than just great taste—they provide essential nutrients tailored to changing dietary needs while simplifying meal preparation.

Olive Oil: The Golden Elixir

- Replaces saturated fats with heart-healthy monounsaturated fats
- Helps reduce LDL ("bad") cholesterol while maintaining HDL ("good") cholesterol (*Cleveland Clinic, 2022*)
- Versatile uses: from salad dressings to gentle sautéing
- Pro tip: Keep a small bottle by the stove for easy access

Fresh Herbs: Nature's Flavor Boosters

- Basil, oregano, and rosemary provide antioxidant and anti-inflammatory benefits
- Allow for reduced sodium intake without sacrificing taste (*Mayo Clinic Staff, 2021*)
- Easy to grow in small kitchen gardens or windowsill pots
- Simple application: toss fresh thyme into roasted vegetables or blend basil into sauces

Seasonal Vegetables: Nutrient-Rich Variety

- Offer peak flavor and nutrition when harvested in season
- Require minimal preparation—often delicious with just olive oil and herbs

Mediterranean Seasonal Produce Guide

Season	Fruits	Vegetables	Legumes/Grains
Spring	Strawberries, Apricots	Artichokes, Asparagus, Peas	Fava beans, Lentils
Summer	Peaches, Figs, Melons	Tomatoes, Zucchini, Eggplant	Chickpeas, Farro
Fall	Pears, Pomegranates	Butternut squash, Mushrooms, Kale	Cannellini beans
Winter	Citrus, Apples	Root vegetables, Cabbage	Split peas, Barley

Seasonal eating ensures optimal nutrient content and reduces cost (Mayo Clinic Staff, 2021). Frozen or canned options (no salt added) make excellent substitutes when fresh isn't available.

Legumes: Plant-Based Protein Powerhouses

- Lentils, chickpeas, and beans provide:
  - High fiber for digestive health
  - Plant protein to maintain muscle mass
  - Iron and B vitamins for energy (*Cleveland Clinic, 2022*)
- Time-saving tip: Use canned varieties (rinsed) for quick meals

Legume Preparation Reference

Legume	Dried (1 cup)	Cooked Yield	Soaking Time	Cooking Time
Lentils	1 cup	2.5 cups	Not required	15-20 min
Chickpeas	1 cup	3 cups	8-12 hours	1-1.5 hours
Black beans	1 cup	3 cups	8-12 hours	45-60 min
Cannellini beans	1 cup	3 cups	8-12 hours	45-60 min

Quick soak method for beans: Cover with boiling water and let stand 1 hour (Cleveland Clinic, 2022). Canned legumes (rinsed) provide equal nutrition in ready-to-use form.

Health Benefits at a Glance

Research confirms Mediterranean ingredients can help:

- Support cardiovascular health
- Maintain healthy blood sugar levels
- Promote beneficial gut bacteria (*Mayo Clinic Staff, 2021*)

Making It Work for You

These ingredients adapt effortlessly to:

- Low-sodium needs (using herbs instead of salt)
- Vegetarian preferences (legumes as protein source)
- Budget considerations (seasonal produce is often more affordable)

By embracing these Mediterranean staples, seniors can transform everyday cooking into a joyful practice that celebrates flavor while supporting long-term wellness. The simplicity of these ingredients belies their profound impact—proving that eating well can be both uncomplicated and deeply satisfying.

Simplicity is the Answer

Our journey through kitchen essentials reveals an important truth: cooking in our later years isn't about limitation—it's about adaptation and rediscovery. With thoughtful tools and smarter strategies, the kitchen transforms from a place of potential frustration to a space of creativity and independence.

The Mediterranean approach offers more than just good nutrition—it brings a philosophy of cooking that celebrates simplicity, flavor, and community. As you incorporate these wholesome ingredients and time-honored techniques, you're not just preparing meals; you're embracing a lifestyle that honors both your changing needs and your enduring love of good food.

May your kitchen continue to be a place of nourishment, discovery, and joy—where every meal celebrates the wisdom of Mediterranean traditions and the pleasure of eating well. Here's to many more delicious, healthful meals shared with those you love.

CHAPTER 3: BREAKFAST

Savory Avocado Toast with Cherry Tomatoes & Olive Oil

Cooking Time: 0 minutes

Prep Time: 10 minutes

Servings: 1

A quick, heart-healthy Mediterranean breakfast that's as delicious as it is nutritious. Rich in healthy fats, fiber, and antioxidants, this simple toast provides a satisfying start to your day—without any fuss. Ideal for supporting heart health, brain function, and steady energy levels.

Ingredients:

- 2 slices whole grain bread (or sprouted grain)
- 1 ripe avocado
- 1/2 cup cherry tomatoes, halved
- 1 tsp extra virgin olive oil
- Pinch of sea salt
- Fresh basil leaves (optional, for garnish)

Instructions:

1. Toast the bread to your desired level of crispiness.
2. While the bread toasts, cut the avocado in half, remove the pit, and scoop the flesh into a small bowl. Mash it lightly with a fork.
3. Spread the mashed avocado evenly onto each slice of toast.
4. Top with halved cherry tomatoes.
5. Drizzle with olive oil and sprinkle a pinch of sea salt.
6. Garnish with fresh basil if desired. Serve immediately.

Nutrition Breakdown (per serving):

- Calories: ~310
- Protein: 6g
- Fat: 21g (mostly monounsaturated)
- Carbohydrates: 28g
- Fiber: 9g
- Sugar: 2g
- Sodium: 180mg
- Potassium: 600mg
- Vitamin C: 20% DV
- Vitamin E: 15% DV

CHAPTER 3: BREAKFAST

Greek Yogurt with Honey, Walnuts & Fresh Berries

 Cooking Time: 0 minutes

 Prep Time: 5 minutes

 Servings: 1

A protein-packed, antioxidant-rich Mediterranean breakfast that supports both heart and brain health. This refreshing and naturally sweet bowl delivers healthy fats, probiotics, and essential nutrients in just minutes—perfect for sustained energy and graceful aging.

Ingredients:

- 1 cup plain Greek yogurt
- 1 tbsp honey
- 1/4 cup walnuts, chopped
- 1/2 cup mixed fresh berries (blueberries, raspberries, strawberries)

Instructions:

1. Scoop the Greek yogurt into a serving bowl.
2. Drizzle the honey evenly over the top.
3. Sprinkle the chopped walnuts on the yogurt.
4. Add the fresh berries on top.
5. Serve immediately, chilled or at room temperature.

Nutrition Breakdown (per serving):

- Calories: ~280
- Protein: 17g
- Fat: 14g
- Carbohydrates: 20g
- Fiber: 3g
- Sugar: 12g
- Sodium: 60mg
- Calcium: 20% DV
- Omega-3s: 5% DV
- Vitamin C: 15% DV

Spinach & Feta Egg Scramble

 Cooking Time: 5 minutes

 Prep Time: 5 minutes

 Servings: 1

A simple one-pan Mediterranean breakfast that comes together in minutes. Packed with protein, leafy greens, and calcium-rich feta, this scramble supports bone health, muscle maintenance, and sustained energy—ideal for seniors seeking a nourishing start to their day.

Ingredients:

- 2 eggs
- 1/2 cup fresh spinach, chopped
- 2 tbsp crumbled feta cheese
- 1 tsp extra virgin olive oil
- Salt and pepper to taste

Instructions:

1. Crack the eggs into a small bowl, add a pinch of salt and pepper, and whisk until well combined.
2. Heat olive oil in a nonstick skillet over medium heat.
3. Add the chopped spinach and sauté for about 1 minute until just wilted.
4. Pour in the eggs and gently stir with a spatula, cooking until softly scrambled.
5. Sprinkle in the feta cheese and cook for 30 seconds more, just until melted slightly.
6. Remove from heat and serve immediately.

Nutrition Breakdown (per serving):

- Calories: ~250
- Protein: 14g
- Fat: 20g
- Carbohydrates: 2g
- Fiber: 0.5g
- Sugar: 1g
- Sodium: 300mg
- Calcium: 15% DV
- Vitamin A: 50% DV
- Iron: 10% DV

CHAPTER 3: BREAKFAST

Mediterranean Oats with Almonds, Dates & Cinnamon

Cooking Time: 5 minutes

Prep Time: 5 minutes

Servings: 1

Quick-cook oats infused with warm spices, naturally sweet dates, and heart-healthy almonds. This comforting Mediterranean breakfast supports digestion, balances blood sugar, and keeps you full and energized throughout the morning.

Ingredients:

- 1/2 cup rolled oats
- 1 cup water or unsweetened almond milk
- 2 dates, chopped
- 1 tbsp sliced almonds
- 1/2 tsp ground cinnamon

Instructions:

1. In a small saucepan, bring the water or almond milk to a gentle boil.
2. Add the oats and reduce heat to a simmer.
3. Stir in the chopped dates and cinnamon.
4. Cook for 4-5 minutes, stirring occasionally, until the oats are soft and creamy.
5. Remove from heat and top with sliced almonds.
6. Serve warm.

Nutrition Breakdown (per serving):

- Calories: ~270
- Protein: 6g
- Fat: 8g
- Carbohydrates: 44g
- Fiber: 6g
- Sugar: 12g
- Sodium: 40mg
- Magnesium: 15% DV
- Iron: 10% DV
- Calcium: 6% DV

Tomato, Basil & Mozzarella Breakfast Sandwich

 Cooking Time: 5 minutes

 Prep Time: 5 minutes

 Servings: 1

A lighter, breakfast-friendly twist on the classic Caprese sandwich. With juicy tomatoes, creamy mozzarella, and fresh basil layered on whole grain bread, this sandwich delivers Mediterranean flavor in a heart-healthy and satisfying way.

Ingredients:

- 1 whole grain English muffin or small whole wheat pita
- 2 slices ripe tomato
- 2 slices fresh mozzarella cheese
- Fresh basil leaves
- Drizzle of extra virgin olive oil
- Pinch of sea salt and cracked black pepper

Instructions:

1. Toast the English muffin or warm the pita until lightly crisp.
2. Layer the tomato slices on one half of the muffin or inside the pita.
3. Add mozzarella slices and fresh basil leaves.
4. Drizzle with olive oil and season with salt and pepper.
5. Close the sandwich and serve warm.

Nutrition Breakdown (per serving):

- Calories: ~310
- Protein: 12g
- Fat: 16g
- Carbohydrates: 28g
- Fiber: 4g
- Sugar: 3g
- Sodium: 300mg
- Calcium: 20% DV
- Vitamin C: 15% DV
- Vitamin A: 10% DV

CHAPTER 3: BREAKFAST

Cucumber, Hummus & Smoked Salmon Wrap

Cooking Time: 0 minutes

Prep Time: 10 minutes

Servings: 1

This no-cook Mediterranean-inspired wrap combines creamy hummus, crisp cucumber, and smoky salmon for a light yet satisfying breakfast. Packed with omega-3s, plant protein, and fiber, it's great for heart health, brain support, and steady morning energy.

Ingredients:

- 1 whole wheat wrap
- 2 tbsp hummus
- 4 slices cucumber
- 2 oz smoked salmon
- Optional: squeeze of lemon juice or a sprinkle of fresh dill

Instructions:

1. Lay the whole wheat wrap flat on a plate or cutting board.
2. Spread the hummus evenly over the surface.
3. Arrange cucumber slices and smoked salmon on top.
4. Add a squeeze of lemon juice or a sprinkle of fresh dill, if using.
5. Roll the wrap tightly and slice in half.
6. Serve chilled or at room temperature.

Nutrition Breakdown (per serving):

- Calories: ~280
- Protein: 15g
- Fat: 14g
- Carbohydrates: 22g
- Fiber: 4g
- Sugar: 2g
- Sodium: 400mg
- Omega-3s: 30% DV
- Vitamin B12: 40% DV
- Iron: 8% DV

Chickpea Breakfast Hash with Bell Peppers & Onions

Cooking Time: 10 minutes
Prep Time: 5 minutes
Servings: 1

Hearty, fiber-rich, and anti-inflammatory, this plant-powered breakfast hash is ideal for gut health and joint support. With colorful veggies and protein-packed chickpeas, it's a warm, savory way to start your day the Mediterranean way.

Ingredients:

- 1/2 cup canned chickpeas, rinsed and drained
- 1/4 cup diced bell pepper (any color)
- 1/4 cup chopped onion
- 1 tsp extra virgin olive oil
- Pinch of ground cumin
- Salt and pepper to taste

Instructions:

1. Heat olive oil in a skillet over medium heat.
2. Add the chopped onion and bell pepper, sautéing for 2-3 minutes until softened.
3. Stir in the chickpeas and cumin.
4. Cook for another 3-4 minutes, stirring occasionally, until everything is warmed through and lightly golden.
5. Season with salt and pepper to taste.
6. Serve hot as is, or with a side of whole grain toast.

Nutrition Breakdown (per serving):

- Calories: ~240
- Protein: 7g
- Fat: 9g
- Carbohydrates: 30g
- Fiber: 7g
- Sugar: 3g
- Sodium: 180mg
- Iron: 15% DV
- Vitamin C: 30% DV
- Magnesium: 10% DV

CHAPTER 3: BREAKFAST

Ricotta & Fig Toast with Walnuts

 Cooking Time: 0 minutes

 Prep Time: 10 minutes

 Servings: 1

A creamy, naturally sweet breakfast packed with Mediterranean flavor. Ricotta provides calcium and protein, while figs offer gut-friendly fiber and a touch of natural sugar. Walnuts round it out with heart-healthy omega-3 fats and satisfying crunch.

Ingredients:

- 2 slices whole grain bread
- 1/4 cup ricotta cheese
- 2 fresh figs (sliced) or 2 dried figs (chopped)
- 1 tbsp chopped walnuts
- Optional: drizzle of honey or sprinkle of cinnamon

Instructions:

1. Toast the slices of whole grain bread to your liking.
2. Spread ricotta cheese evenly on each slice.
3. Top with fresh or dried figs.
4. Sprinkle with chopped walnuts.
5. Add a light drizzle of honey or a dash of cinnamon if desired.
6. Serve immediately.

Nutrition Breakdown (per serving):

- Calories: ~320
- Protein: 11g
- Fat: 15g
- Carbohydrates: 35g
- Fiber: 5g
- Sugar: 8g
- Sodium: 180mg
- Calcium: 20% DV
- Potassium: 10% DV
- Zinc: 8% DV

Mediterranean Smoothie with Spinach, Banana & Olive Oil

Cooking Time: 0 minutes
Prep Time: 5 minutes
Servings: 1

A refreshing and nutrient-dense smoothie that supports anti-inflammatory health and muscle function. This Mediterranean-inspired blend is rich in fiber, potassium, healthy fats, and antioxidants—perfect for a light, energizing breakfast or mid-morning boost.

Ingredients:

- 1/2 banana
- 1/2 cup fresh spinach
- 1/2 cup plain Greek yogurt
- 1/2 cup water
- 1 tsp extra virgin olive oil
- A few ice cubes
- Optional: squeeze of lemon or pinch of cinnamon

Instructions:

1. Add the banana, spinach, yogurt, water, olive oil, and ice cubes to a blender.
2. Blend on high speed until smooth and creamy.
3. Taste and adjust with lemon or cinnamon, if desired.
4. Pour into a glass and enjoy immediately.

Nutrition Breakdown (per serving):

- Calories: ~220
- Protein: 10g
- Fat: 9g
- Carbohydrates: 22g
- Fiber: 3g
- Sugar: 10g
- Sodium: 50mg
- Potassium: 450mg
- Vitamin K: 60% DV
- Vitamin C: 20% DV

CHAPTER 3: BREAKFAST

Poached Eggs with Sauteed Kale & Garlic

 Cooking Time: 5 minutes

 Prep Time: 5 minutes

 Servings: 1

A nourishing, protein-rich breakfast with leafy greens and a Mediterranean twist. This simple dish delivers brain-boosting choline, bone-supporting vitamin K, and anti-inflammatory benefits in under 10 minutes—ideal for seniors looking for strength and simplicity.

Ingredients:

- 2 eggs
- 1/2 cup chopped kale (stems removed)
- 1 clove garlic, minced
- 1 tsp extra virgin olive oil
- Pinch of sea salt and black pepper
- Optional: dash of red pepper flakes or squeeze of lemon

Instructions:

1. Fill a small pot with water and bring to a gentle simmer for poaching.
2. While the water heats, warm olive oil in a skillet over medium heat.
3. Add garlic and sauté for 30 seconds, then add kale and cook for 2-3 minutes until wilted.
4. Crack each egg into a small cup, then gently lower into the simmering water.
5. Poach eggs for 3-4 minutes until whites are set but yolks are still soft.
6. Remove with a slotted spoon and place on top of the sautéed kale.
7. Season with salt and pepper. Add optional red pepper flakes or lemon if desired.

Nutrition Breakdown (per serving):

- Calories: ~210
- Protein: 14g
- Fat: 15g
- Carbohydrates: 4g
- Fiber: 1g
- Sugar: 1g
- Sodium: 160mg
- Vitamin K: 100% DV
- Vitamin A: 45% DV
- Choline: 50% DV

Warm Quinoa Breakfast Bowl with Almond Milk & Berries

 Cooking Time: 5 minutes (using pre-cooked quinoa)

 Prep Time: 5 minutes

 Servings: 1

A plant-based, gluten-free breakfast bowl full of complete protein, fiber, and antioxidants. This warm, comforting dish supports heart health, digestion, and sustained energy—an excellent Mediterranean option for seniors looking for gentle nourishment.

Ingredients:

- 1/2 cup cooked quinoa
- 1/2 cup unsweetened almond milk
- 1/2 cup fresh berries (blueberries, raspberries, or sliced strawberries)
- 1 tbsp sliced almonds
- Optional: 1/2 tsp cinnamon or drizzle of maple syrup

Instructions:

1. In a small saucepan, combine cooked quinoa and almond milk.
2. Warm over medium heat for 3-5 minutes, stirring occasionally, until heated through.
3. Transfer to a bowl and top with fresh berries and sliced almonds.
4. Add cinnamon or a light drizzle of maple syrup, if desired.
5. Serve warm.

Nutrition Breakdown (per serving):

- Calories: ~260
- Protein: 8g
- Fat: 9g
- Carbohydrates: 34g
- Fiber: 5g
- Sugar: 6g
- Sodium: 60mg
- Iron: 15% DV
- Magnesium: 20% DV
- Vitamin C: 10% DV

CHAPTER 3: BREAKFAST

Zucchini & Herb Omelette with Goat Cheese

 Cooking Time: 5 minutes

 Prep Time: 5 minutes

 Servings: 1

Light, fresh, and full of Mediterranean flavor, this omelette is easy to digest and packed with nutrients. Zucchini provides hydration and fiber, while herbs and creamy goat cheese add flavor and elegance to this senior-friendly breakfast.

Ingredients:

- 2 eggs
- 1/4 cup grated zucchini (squeezed dry)
- 1 tbsp chopped fresh herbs (parsley, dill, or basil)
- 1 tbsp goat cheese
- 1 tsp extra virgin olive oil
- Salt and pepper to taste

Instructions:

1. Crack the eggs into a bowl, add salt and pepper, and whisk until well combined.
2. Heat olive oil in a nonstick skillet over medium heat.
3. Add the grated zucchini and sauté for 1–2 minutes until softened.
4. Pour the eggs over the zucchini and cook undisturbed for 1 minute.
5. Sprinkle in the chopped herbs and goat cheese.
6. Once the bottom is set, gently fold the omelette in half and cook for another 1–2 minutes.
7. Serve hot.

Nutrition Breakdown (per serving):

- Calories: ~230
- Protein: 13g
- Fat: 18g
- Carbohydrates: 3g
- Fiber: 1g
- Sugar: 1g
- Sodium: 220mg
- Calcium: 10% DV
- Vitamin A: 25% DV
- Folate: 15% DV

Apple-Cinnamon Chia Pudding (Prepped the Night Before)

 Cooking Time: 0 minutes

 Prep Time: 5 minutes (plus overnight chill)

 Servings: 1

A make-ahead Mediterranean breakfast that's rich in fiber, omega-3s, and plant-based protein. This apple-cinnamon chia pudding is perfect for seniors seeking a gut-friendly, blood sugar–balancing option that requires no morning effort.

Ingredients:

- 3 tbsp chia seeds
- 1/2 cup unsweetened almond milk
- 1/4 apple, finely diced
- 1/4 tsp ground cinnamon
- 1 tsp maple syrup or honey (optional)

Instructions:

1. In a small jar or bowl, combine chia seeds, almond milk, diced apple, cinnamon, and maple syrup (if using).
2. Stir well to prevent clumping.
3. Cover and refrigerate overnight, or for at least 4 hours.
4. In the morning, stir again and add a splash of milk if needed for consistency.
5. Serve chilled.

Nutrition Breakdown (per serving):

- Calories: ~210
- Protein: 5g
- Fat: 9g
- Carbohydrates: 27g
- Fiber: 9g
- Sugar: 10g
- Sodium: 70mg
- Omega-3s: 50% DV
- Calcium: 15% DV
- Magnesium: 20% DV

CHAPTER 3: BREAKFAST

Whole Grain Pita with Hummus, Sliced Egg & Cucumber

 Cooking Time: 0 minutes

 Prep Time: 10 minutes

 Servings: 1

This no-cook Mediterranean breakfast is balanced, protein-rich, and perfect for seniors on the go. Creamy hummus, hearty egg, and crisp cucumber come together in a fiber-packed whole grain pita for a satisfying and nourishing start to your day.

Ingredients:

- 1 whole grain pita pocket
- 2 tbsp hummus
- 1 hard-boiled egg, sliced
- 4-6 slices cucumber
- Optional: pinch of paprika or fresh herbs for garnish

Instructions:

1. Cut the pita in half to create two pockets.
2. Spread 1 tbsp of hummus inside each half.
3. Add slices of hard-boiled egg and cucumber.
4. Sprinkle with paprika or chopped herbs, if desired.
5. Serve chilled or at room temperature.

Nutrition Breakdown (per serving):

- Calories: ~250
- Protein: 11g
- Fat: 12g
- Carbohydrates: 25g
- Fiber: 5g
- Sugar: 1g
- Sodium: 240mg
- Folate: 10% DV
- Vitamin B12: 15% DV
- Iron: 10% DV

Red Pepper & Goat Cheese Breakfast Wrap

Cooking Time: 5 minutes
Prep Time: 5 minutes
Servings: 1

A flavorful and filling Mediterranean-style breakfast that wraps up creamy goat cheese, sautéed red pepper, and soft scrambled eggs in a whole wheat tortilla. This wrap is rich in protein, calcium, and antioxidants—perfect for boosting morning energy and supporting healthy aging.

Ingredients:

- 1 whole wheat tortilla
- 2 eggs
- 2 tbsp crumbled goat cheese
- 1/4 cup diced red bell pepper
- 1 tsp extra virgin olive oil
- Salt and pepper to taste

Instructions:

1. Heat olive oil in a skillet over medium heat.
2. Add the diced red bell pepper and sauté for 2 minutes, until slightly softened.
3. In a bowl, whisk the eggs with a pinch of salt and pepper.
4. Pour the eggs into the skillet with the peppers and scramble gently until just set.
5. Stir in the goat cheese and remove from heat.
6. Spoon the mixture into the tortilla, roll it up tightly, and slice in half.
7. Serve warm.

Nutrition Breakdown (per serving):

- Calories: ~310
- Protein: 16g
- Fat: 19g
- Carbohydrates: 22g
- Fiber: 3g
- Sugar: 2g
- Sodium: 280mg
- Vitamin A: 30% DV
- Calcium: 15% DV
- Iron: 10% DV

Mediterranean Cottage Cheese Bowl

 Cooking Time: 0 minutes

 Prep Time: 5 minutes

 Servings: 1

A refreshing, protein-rich breakfast bowl that's savory, satisfying, and quick to assemble. Cottage cheese pairs beautifully with hydrating veggies and briny olives—making it a great low-sugar option for supporting muscle strength, heart health, and hydration.

Ingredients:

- 1 cup low-fat cottage cheese
- 1/2 cup cherry tomatoes, halved
- 1/4 cucumber, thinly sliced
- 1 tbsp kalamata olives, sliced
- 1 tsp extra virgin olive oil
- Fresh dill or parsley for garnish

Instructions:

1. Scoop the cottage cheese into a serving bowl.
2. Arrange the cherry tomatoes, cucumber slices, and olives on top.
3. Drizzle with olive oil.
4. Garnish with chopped fresh dill or parsley.
5. Serve immediately.

Nutrition Breakdown (per serving):

- Calories: ~220
- Protein: 20g
- Fat: 10g
- Carbohydrates: 8g
- Fiber: 1g
- Sugar: 4g
- Sodium: 380mg
- Calcium: 15% DV
- Vitamin C: 10% DV
- Potassium: 8% DV

Almond Butter & Banana Toast with Chia Seeds

Cooking Time: 0 minutes

Prep Time: 5 minutes

Servings: 1

A quick and energizing Mediterranean-inspired breakfast that combines healthy fats, fiber, and potassium. This toast supports heart health, digestion, and steady blood sugar—perfect for seniors needing a simple yet nourishing start to the day.

Ingredients:

- 1 slice whole grain bread
- 1 tbsp almond butter
- 1/2 banana, sliced
- 1/2 tsp chia seeds
- Dash of cinnamon (optional)

Instructions:

1. Toast the slice of whole grain bread to your desired crispness.
2. Spread the almond butter evenly over the warm toast.
3. Top with banana slices.
4. Sprinkle with chia seeds.
5. Add a dash of cinnamon, if desired.
6. Serve immediately.

Nutrition Breakdown (per serving):

- Calories: ~270
- Protein: 6g
- Fat: 14g
- Carbohydrates: 30g
- Fiber: 5g
- Sugar: 9g
- Sodium: 120mg
- Potassium: 350mg
- Vitamin E: 20% DV
- Magnesium: 10% DV

CHAPTER 3: BREAKFAST

Herbed Tomato & Egg Skillet

Cooking Time: 6 minutes

Prep Time: 4 minutes

Servings: 1

A rustic, one-pan Mediterranean breakfast that's simple, satisfying, and packed with flavor. Juicy tomatoes and herbs combine with protein-rich eggs for a quick dish that supports heart health, vision, and brain function—all in under 10 minutes.

Ingredients:

- 2 eggs
- 1/2 cup cherry tomatoes, halved
- 1/4 tsp dried oregano
- 1 tsp extra virgin olive oil
- Salt and pepper to taste
- Optional: crumbled feta or chopped parsley for garnish

Instructions:

1. Heat olive oil in a small skillet over medium heat.
2. Add cherry tomatoes and oregano; sauté for 2-3 minutes, until tomatoes soften and release some juices.
3. Crack the eggs directly into the skillet, spaced slightly apart.
4. Sprinkle with salt and pepper.
5. Cover the skillet with a lid and cook for 3-4 minutes, or until the egg whites are set and yolks are cooked to your liking.
6. Garnish with crumbled feta or fresh parsley, if using.
7. Serve warm.

Nutrition Breakdown (per serving):

- Calories: ~230
- Protein: 13g
- Fat: 18g
- Carbohydrates: 4g
- Fiber: 1g
- Sugar: 2g
- Sodium: 160mg
- Vitamin C: 20% DV
- Vitamin A: 30% DV
- Iron: 10% DV

Apricot & Walnut Greek Yogurt Bowl

Cooking Time: 0 minutes

Prep Time: 5 minutes

Servings: 1

This creamy, tangy bowl combines the gut-friendly benefits of Greek yogurt with the brain-boosting power of walnuts and the natural sweetness of apricots. It's a Mediterranean-inspired breakfast that supports digestion, focus, and energy without the need to cook.

Ingredients:

- 1 cup plain Greek yogurt
- 2 dried apricots, chopped
- 1 tbsp chopped walnuts
- 1 tsp honey (optional)
- Sprinkle of cinnamon

Instructions:

1. Scoop the Greek yogurt into a serving bowl.
2. Top with chopped dried apricots and walnuts.
3. Drizzle with honey, if desired.
4. Finish with a light sprinkle of cinnamon.
5. Serve chilled.

Nutrition Breakdown (per serving):

- Calories: ~290
- Protein: 17g
- Fat: 12g
- Carbohydrates: 25g
- Fiber: 2g
- Sugar: 14g
- Sodium: 50mg
- Calcium: 20% DV
- Omega-3s: 5% DV
- Zinc: 8% DV

CHAPTER 4: LUNCH

Grilled Chicken Shawarma Bowl

 Cooking Time: 15 minutes

 Prep Time: 10 minutes (plus marinating time)

 Servings: 2

A flavorful and nourishing Mediterranean lunch featuring spiced grilled chicken served over a bed of brown rice with crunchy cucumbers, juicy tomatoes, and a creamy tahini drizzle. This balanced bowl is high in protein, fiber, and heart-healthy fats—perfect for seniors seeking both taste and vitality.

Ingredients:

For the Chicken Marinade:
- 2 boneless, skinless chicken thighs (or breasts)
- 1 tbsp olive oil
- 1 tsp ground cumin
- 1 tsp smoked paprika
- 1/2 tsp ground turmeric
- 1/4 tsp cinnamon
- 1/4 tsp garlic powder
- Salt and pepper to taste
- Juice of 1/2 lemon

For the Bowl:
- 1 cup cooked brown rice
- 1/2 cup chopped cucumber
- 1/2 cup chopped tomato
- 2 tbsp chopped parsley

Tahini Sauce:
- 2 tbsp tahini
- 1 tbsp lemon juice
- 1 tbsp water (more as needed)
- 1/2 clove garlic, minced
- Pinch of salt

Instructions:

1. In a bowl, whisk together all marinade ingredients. Add the chicken, coat well, and marinate for at least 30 minutes (or up to 8 hours).
2. Heat a grill pan or skillet over medium heat. Cook chicken for 5-7 minutes per side, or until fully cooked and golden brown. Let rest, then slice.
3. In a small bowl, whisk together the tahini sauce ingredients until smooth. Add more water for desired consistency.
4. To assemble the bowl, divide brown rice into two bowls. Top each with sliced chicken, cucumbers, tomatoes, and parsley.
5. Drizzle with tahini sauce and serve warm or at room temperature.

Nutrition Breakdown (per serving):

- Calories: ~420
- Protein: 28g
- Fat: 20g
- Carbohydrates: 32g
- Fiber: 6g
- Sugar: 3g
- Sodium: 280mg
- Iron: 15% DV
- Vitamin C: 20% DV
- Magnesium: 10% DV

CHAPTER 4: LUNCH

Mediterranean Lentil Salad

 Cooking Time: 20 minutes (for lentils)

 Prep Time: 10 minutes

 Servings: 2

A refreshing, protein-packed salad made with tender lentils, crisp vegetables, and a bright lemon-herb vinaigrette. This fiber-rich dish supports heart health, blood sugar balance, and digestion—making it a perfect midday meal for seniors.

Ingredients:

For the Salad:

- 1 cup cooked green or brown lentils (about 1/2 cup dry)
- 1/2 cup cherry tomatoes, halved
- 1/2 cup cucumber, diced
- 1/4 cup red onion, finely chopped
- 2 tbsp chopped fresh parsley
- 1 tbsp crumbled feta cheese (optional)

For the Dressing:

- 2 tbsp extra virgin olive oil
- Juice of 1 lemon
- 1/2 tsp dried oregano
- Salt and pepper to taste

Instructions:

1. Cook lentils according to package instructions until tender but not mushy (usually about 15–20 minutes). Drain and cool slightly.
2. In a large bowl, combine cooked lentils, cherry tomatoes, cucumber, red onion, and parsley.
3. In a small jar or bowl, whisk together olive oil, lemon juice, oregano, salt, and pepper.
4. Pour the dressing over the lentil mixture and toss to combine.
5. Top with crumbled feta, if using. Serve immediately or refrigerate and enjoy chilled.

Nutrition Breakdown (per serving):

- Calories: ~320
- Protein: 15g
- Fat: 14g
- Carbohydrates: 35g
- Fiber: 12g
- Sugar: 4g
- Sodium: 220mg
- Iron: 25% DV
- Folate: 50% DV
- Vitamin C: 10% DV

Tuna & White Bean Salad

Cooking Time: 0 minutes
Prep Time: 10 minutes
Servings: 2

This no-cook Mediterranean lunch is light, protein-rich, and loaded with omega-3s. Creamy white beans and tender tuna are paired with peppery arugula and bright lemon-olive oil dressing, making it a perfect option for supporting heart and brain health in a senior-friendly way.

Ingredients:

- 1 (5 oz) can tuna in olive oil, drained
- 1 cup canned white beans (like cannellini or great northern), rinsed and drained
- 1 cup arugula or baby spinach
- 1/2 cup cherry tomatoes, halved
- 1 tbsp capers (optional)
- 2 tbsp chopped red onion
- 2 tbsp extra virgin olive oil
- Juice of 1/2 lemon
- Salt and pepper to taste

Instructions:

1. In a medium bowl, flake the tuna with a fork.
2. Add the white beans, arugula, cherry tomatoes, red onion, and capers (if using).
3. Drizzle with olive oil and lemon juice.
4. Gently toss everything together until well combined.
5. Season with salt and pepper to taste. Serve immediately or chill for later.

Nutrition Breakdown (per serving):

- Calories: ~350
- Protein: 22g
- Fat: 18g
- Carbohydrates: 24g
- Fiber: 6g
- Sugar: 2g
- Sodium: 350mg
- Omega-3s: 30% DV
- Iron: 20% DV
- Folate: 15% DV

CHAPTER 4: LUNCH

Stuffed Bell Peppers with Quinoa & Feta

 Cooking Time: 25 minutes

 Prep Time: 10 minutes

 Servings: 2

These vibrant stuffed peppers are filled with a Mediterranean blend of herbed quinoa, chickpeas, spinach, and creamy feta. Packed with fiber, plant-based protein, and antioxidants, they're a colorful and heart-healthy lunch option—perfect for supporting digestion and energy.

Ingredients:

- 2 large bell peppers, halved and seeds removed
- 1 cup cooked quinoa
- 1/2 cup canned chickpeas, rinsed and mashed slightly
- 1 cup baby spinach, chopped
- 1/4 cup crumbled feta cheese
- 1 tbsp chopped fresh parsley
- 1 tbsp olive oil
- 1/2 tsp dried oregano
- Salt and pepper to taste
- Optional: squeeze of lemon juice

Instructions:

1. Preheat oven to 375°F (190°C). Lightly grease a small baking dish.
2. In a bowl, combine cooked quinoa, mashed chickpeas, chopped spinach, feta, parsley, olive oil, oregano, salt, and pepper. Mix well.
3. Stuff each bell pepper half with the quinoa mixture and place in the baking dish.
4. Cover with foil and bake for 20 minutes. Uncover and bake an additional 5 minutes until peppers are tender and tops are slightly golden.
5. Optional: squeeze fresh lemon juice over the top before serving.

Nutrition Breakdown (per serving):

- Calories: ~360
- Protein: 14g
- Fat: 16g
- Carbohydrates: 38g
- Fiber: 8g
- Sugar: 6g
- Sodium: 280mg
- Vitamin C: 150% DV
- Iron: 20% DV
- Calcium: 15% DV

Baked Falafel Lettuce Wraps

 Cooking Time: 20 minutes

 Prep Time: 10 minutes

 Servings: 2

These oven-baked falafel lettuce wraps are crisp on the outside, tender on the inside, and bursting with Mediterranean flavor. Served in fresh lettuce leaves with tzatziki and shredded veggies, this lunch is fiber-rich, anti-inflammatory, and easy on digestion—great for seniors looking for a lighter, satisfying option.

Ingredients:

For the Falafel:
- 1 cup canned chickpeas, rinsed and patted dry
- 1 clove garlic
- 2 tbsp chopped parsley
- 1 tbsp chopped red onion
- 1 tbsp olive oil (plus more for baking)
- 1 tbsp oat flour or whole wheat flour
- 1/2 tsp ground cumin
- 1/4 tsp ground coriander
- Salt and pepper to taste

For Serving:
- 6 large butter or romaine lettuce leaves
- 1/2 cup shredded carrots or red cabbage
- 1/4 cup chopped cucumber
- 1/4 cup tzatziki sauce (store-bought or homemade)

Instructions:

1. Preheat oven to 400°F (200°C). Line a baking sheet with parchment paper.
2. In a food processor, combine all falafel ingredients. Pulse until crumbly but able to hold together when pressed. Don't overblend.
3. Form into 6 small patties and place on the baking sheet. Lightly brush or spray with olive oil.
4. Bake for 10 minutes, flip, and bake another 8-10 minutes until golden and firm.
5. Let cool slightly. Then, place 1 falafel in each lettuce leaf, top with shredded veggies and cucumber, and drizzle with tzatziki.
6. Serve immediately.

Nutrition Breakdown (per serving):

- Calories: ~300
- Protein: 11g
- Fat: 14g
- Carbohydrates: 30g
- Fiber: 7g
- Sugar: 3g
- Sodium: 240mg
- Folate: 30% DV
- Vitamin K: 70% DV
- Iron: 15% DV

CHAPTER 4: LUNCH

Zucchini Noodles with Pesto & Cherry Tomatoes

 Cooking Time: 5 minutes

 Prep Time: 10 minutes

 Servings: 2

A light, refreshing, and low-carb Mediterranean lunch perfect for warm days. These zucchini noodles are tossed in a flavorful basil pesto and paired with sweet cherry tomatoes, offering healthy fats, antioxidants, and plenty of fiber—ideal for digestion and blood sugar balance.

Ingredients:

- 2 medium zucchinis, spiralized into noodles (or use pre-spiralized)
- 1/2 cup cherry tomatoes, halved
- 1/4 cup basil pesto (store-bought or homemade)
- 1 tsp olive oil
- Salt and pepper to taste
- Optional: 1 tbsp grated Parmesan cheese or crumbled feta

Instructions:

1. Heat olive oil in a large skillet over medium heat.
2. Add the zucchini noodles and sauté for 2-3 minutes, just until slightly tender but not mushy.
3. Add the cherry tomatoes and cook 1-2 minutes more, until warmed through.
4. Remove from heat and toss with pesto. Mix until evenly coated.
5. Season with salt and pepper to taste.
6. Sprinkle with cheese or feta if desired. Serve immediately.

Nutrition Breakdown (per serving):

- Calories: ~220
- Protein: 5g
- Fat: 17g
- Carbohydrates: 11g
- Fiber: 3g
- Sugar: 6g
- Sodium: 250mg
- Vitamin A: 25% DV
- Vitamin C: 35% DV
- Magnesium: 10% DV

Grilled Eggplant & Chickpea Wrap

 Cooking Time: 10 minutes

 Prep Time: 10 minutes

 Servings: 2

This hearty vegetarian wrap features smoky grilled eggplant, creamy chickpeas, and a drizzle of tahini sauce—all rolled into a whole wheat wrap. It's rich in fiber, plant protein, and antioxidants, making it a satisfying and heart-healthy Mediterranean lunch option for seniors.

Ingredients:

- 1 small eggplant, sliced into 1/4-inch rounds
- 1/2 cup canned chickpeas, rinsed and lightly mashed
- 2 whole wheat wraps
- 1/4 cup shredded lettuce or baby spinach
- 1/4 cup chopped cucumber
- 2 tbsp tahini
- 1 tbsp lemon juice
- 1 tsp olive oil
- Salt and pepper to taste
- Optional: pinch of cumin or smoked paprika

Instructions:

1. Brush eggplant slices with olive oil and season with salt and pepper.
2. Grill or cook on a skillet over medium-high heat for 3-4 minutes per side until tender and golden. Set aside.
3. In a small bowl, mix tahini with lemon juice, a splash of water, and a pinch of salt until smooth and pourable.
4. To assemble the wraps, layer mashed chickpeas, grilled eggplant, cucumber, and greens onto each wrap.
5. Drizzle with tahini sauce. Add cumin or paprika if desired.
6. Roll tightly and slice in half. Serve warm or at room temperature.

Nutrition Breakdown (per serving):

- Calories: ~330
- Protein: 10g
- Fat: 16g
- Carbohydrates: 38g
- Fiber: 8g
- Sugar: 4g
- Sodium: 240mg
- Potassium: 15% DV
- Iron: 15% DV
- Folate: 20% DV

CHAPTER 4: LUNCH

Salmon & Farro Grain Bowl

Cooking Time: 10 minutes (using pre-cooked salmon and farro)

Prep Time: 10 minutes

Servings: 2

This nourishing bowl combines hearty farro, flaky salmon, and fresh Mediterranean veggies with a zesty lemon-olive oil dressing. Packed with omega-3s, fiber, and complex carbs, it supports brain function, heart health, and steady energy—ideal for seniors.

Ingredients:

- 1 cup cooked farro
- 1 cup cooked salmon (grilled, baked, or canned), flaked
- 1/2 cup arugula or baby spinach
- 1/4 cup chopped cucumber
- 1/4 cup cherry tomatoes, halved
- 2 tbsp kalamata olives, sliced
- 2 tbsp chopped parsley or dill

For the Dressing:
- 2 tbsp extra virgin olive oil
- Juice of 1/2 lemon
- 1/2 tsp Dijon mustard
- Salt and pepper to taste

Instructions:

1. In a large bowl, combine farro, flaked salmon, arugula, cucumber, tomatoes, olives, and herbs.
2. In a small jar or bowl, whisk together olive oil, lemon juice, Dijon mustard, salt, and pepper.
3. Drizzle the dressing over the bowl and toss gently to combine.
4. Serve chilled or at room temperature.

Nutrition Breakdown (per serving):

- Calories: ~410
- Protein: 25g
- Fat: 20g
- Carbohydrates: 32g
- Fiber: 6g
- Sugar: 3g
- Sodium: 320mg
- Omega-3s: 60% DV
- Vitamin D: 70% DV
- Iron: 15% DV

Mediterranean Turkey Burger

Cooking Time: 12 minutes
Prep Time: 10 minutes
Servings: 2

These lean turkey burgers are packed with Mediterranean herbs and garlic, then topped with creamy hummus and crisp cucumber. High in protein and low in saturated fat, they're a flavorful and joint-friendly lunch option for seniors that supports lean muscle and heart health.

Ingredients:

For the Patties:
- 1/2 lb ground turkey (93% lean)
- 1 clove garlic, minced
- 1 tbsp chopped fresh parsley or 1 tsp dried oregano
- 1/4 tsp ground cumin
- 1/4 tsp salt
- Black pepper to taste
- 1 tsp olive oil (for cooking)

For Serving:
- 2 whole wheat burger buns or sandwich thins
- 2 tbsp hummus
- 1/4 cup cucumber, thinly sliced
- Optional: tomato slices, red onion, lettuce

Instructions:

1. In a bowl, combine ground turkey, garlic, herbs, cumin, salt, and pepper. Mix gently and form into 2 patties.
2. Heat olive oil in a nonstick skillet over medium heat.
3. Cook patties for 5–6 minutes per side, or until fully cooked through (internal temp 165°F).
4. Toast the buns if desired. Spread 1 tbsp hummus on each bun.
5. Place turkey patties on buns and top with cucumber and any optional toppings.
6. Serve warm.

Nutrition Breakdown (per serving):

- Calories: ~360
- Protein: 28g
- Fat: 16g
- Carbohydrates: 26g
- Fiber: 4g
- Sugar: 3g
- Sodium: 330mg
- Vitamin B6: 30% DV
- Zinc: 25% DV
- Iron: 15% DV

CHAPTER 4: LUNCH

Greek Chickpea Stew

 Cooking Time: 25 minutes

 Prep Time: 10 minutes

 Servings: 2

A warming, hearty Mediterranean stew featuring chickpeas, tomatoes, garlic, and fresh spinach. Infused with herbs and a splash of lemon, this comforting dish is perfect for seniors looking for a nutritious, plant-based lunch that supports digestion, heart health, and overall well-being.

Ingredients:

- 1 tbsp extra virgin olive oil
- 1 medium onion, chopped
- 2 garlic cloves, minced
- 1 can (14.5 oz) diced tomatoes
- 1 can (15 oz) chickpeas, drained and rinsed
- 1 cup low-sodium vegetable broth (or water)
- 1/2 tsp dried oregano
- 1/4 tsp dried thyme
- Juice of 1/2 lemon
- 1 cup baby spinach
- Salt and pepper to taste
- Optional: crumbled feta cheese for garnish

Instructions:

1. In a large saucepan, heat the olive oil over medium heat. Add the chopped onion and sauté until soft and translucent, about 4-5 minutes.
2. Stir in the minced garlic and cook for another 30 seconds until fragrant.
3. Add the diced tomatoes (with their juices), chickpeas, and vegetable broth to the saucepan.
4. Sprinkle in the dried oregano and thyme, then bring the mixture to a simmer. Allow it to cook for about 15 minutes to blend the flavors.
5. Stir in the baby spinach and lemon juice, and let the stew simmer for an additional 2 minutes until the spinach wilts.
6. Season with salt and pepper to taste, and garnish with crumbled feta cheese if desired. Serve warm.

Nutrition Breakdown (per serving):

- Calories: ~300
- Protein: 12g
- Fat: 10g
- Carbohydrates: 40g
- Fiber: 10g
- Sugar: 8g
- Sodium: 400mg
- Vitamin C: 40% DV
- Iron: 15% DV
- Calcium: 10% DV

Caprese Quinoa Bowl

Cooking Time: 15 minutes (for quinoa)

Prep Time: 5 minutes

Servings: 2

This vibrant and refreshing grain bowl is a Mediterranean twist on the classic Caprese salad. Protein-rich quinoa is paired with juicy tomatoes, creamy mozzarella, and fragrant basil—all finished with a drizzle of balsamic glaze. It's light, anti-inflammatory, and ideal for supporting energy and blood sugar balance.

Ingredients:

- 1 cup cooked quinoa (from 1/2 cup dry)
- 1 cup cherry tomatoes, halved
- 1/2 cup mozzarella pearls or diced fresh mozzarella
- 1/4 cup chopped fresh basil
- 2 tbsp extra virgin olive oil
- 1 tbsp balsamic glaze or vinegar
- Salt and pepper to taste

Instructions:

1. If not already done, cook quinoa according to package directions. Fluff with a fork and let cool slightly.
2. In a large bowl, combine quinoa, cherry tomatoes, mozzarella, and basil.
3. Drizzle with olive oil and balsamic glaze or vinegar.
4. Season with salt and pepper, then gently toss to combine.
5. Serve immediately or refrigerate and enjoy chilled.

Nutrition Breakdown (per serving):

- Calories: ~340
- Protein: 13g
- Fat: 18g
- Carbohydrates: 30g
- Fiber: 4g
- Sugar: 4g
- Sodium: 220mg
- Calcium: 15% DV
- Vitamin C: 20% DV
- Magnesium: 10% DV

CHAPTER 4: LUNCH

Herbed Chicken Pita Pocket

 Cooking Time: 10 minutes (for chicken)

 Prep Time: 10 minutes

 Servings: 2

This quick and flavorful lunch features tender herbed chicken tucked inside whole wheat pita with creamy tzatziki, crisp lettuce, and juicy tomato. High in protein and full of Mediterranean flavor, it's ideal for supporting muscle strength and energy—perfect for seniors on the go.

Ingredients:

- 1 small boneless, skinless chicken breast
- 1 tsp olive oil
- 1/2 tsp dried oregano
- 1/4 tsp garlic powder
- Salt and pepper to taste
- 1 whole wheat pita, halved
- 1/4 cup tzatziki sauce (store-bought or homemade)
- 1/2 cup shredded lettuce
- 1 small tomato, sliced

Instructions:

1. Pound chicken breast to even thickness. Rub with olive oil, oregano, garlic powder, salt, and pepper.
2. Cook chicken in a skillet over medium heat for about 4-5 minutes per side, or until fully cooked. Let rest, then slice thinly.
3. Open each pita half and spread 1-2 tbsp tzatziki inside.
4. Layer in the sliced chicken, shredded lettuce, and tomato slices.
5. Serve warm or cold.

Nutrition Breakdown (per serving):

- Calories: ~330
- Protein: 26g
- Fat: 13g
- Carbohydrates: 28g
- Fiber: 4g
- Sugar: 2g
- Sodium: 320mg
- Vitamin A: 20% DV
- Calcium: 10% DV
- Iron: 12% DV

Shrimp & Orzo Salad

Cooking Time: 10 minutes

Prep Time: 10 minutes

Servings: 2

A light and zesty Mediterranean pasta salad featuring tender shrimp, briny olives, crisp cucumbers, and a refreshing lemon-dill dressing. This dish is rich in protein, low in saturated fat, and perfect for supporting heart and joint health in seniors.

Ingredients:

- 1/2 cup dry orzo (about 1 cup cooked)
- 6-8 medium shrimp, peeled and deveined
- 1/2 cup chopped cucumber
- 1/4 cup cherry tomatoes, halved
- 2 tbsp chopped kalamata olives
- 1 tbsp chopped fresh dill
- 1 tbsp olive oil
- Juice of 1/2 lemon
- Salt and pepper to taste
- Optional: crumbled feta cheese

Instructions:

1. Cook orzo according to package instructions. Drain, rinse with cool water, and set aside.
2. Season shrimp with a pinch of salt and pepper. Sauté in a skillet with a little olive oil over medium heat until pink and cooked through (about 2-3 minutes per side).
3. In a large bowl, combine cooked orzo, shrimp, cucumber, tomatoes, olives, and dill.
4. Drizzle with olive oil and lemon juice. Toss gently to combine.
5. Top with crumbled feta, if using. Serve chilled or at room temperature.

Nutrition Breakdown (per serving):

- Calories: ~340
- Protein: 24g
- Fat: 14g
- Carbohydrates: 30g
- Fiber: 3g
- Sugar: 2g
- Sodium: 340mg
- Omega-3s: 25% DV
- Vitamin B12: 35% DV
- Iron: 10% DV

CHAPTER 4: LUNCH

Vegetable & Feta Stuffed Pita

Cooking Time: 5–7 minutes (for sautéed vegetables)

Prep Time: 10 minutes

Servings: 2

A warm, satisfying vegetarian lunch featuring sautéed Mediterranean vegetables and tangy feta, all tucked into a whole wheat pita. This easy, fiber-rich meal supports digestive health, brain function, and energy—perfect for seniors seeking something nourishing and quick.

Ingredients:

- 1 whole wheat pita, halved
- 1/2 zucchini, diced
- 1/2 red bell pepper, diced
- 1/4 small red onion, thinly sliced
- 1 tbsp olive oil
- 1/4 tsp dried oregano
- Salt and pepper to taste
- 1/4 cup crumbled feta cheese
- Optional: fresh parsley for garnish

Instructions:

1. Heat olive oil in a skillet over medium heat. Add zucchini, red bell pepper, and red onion.
2. Sauté for 5–7 minutes until vegetables are tender and slightly caramelized.
3. Season with oregano, salt, and pepper.
4. Stuff each pita half with the sautéed veggies and top with crumbled feta.
5. Garnish with chopped parsley, if desired. Serve warm.

Nutrition Breakdown (per serving):

- Calories: ~310
- Protein: 9g
- Fat: 16g
- Carbohydrates: 32g
- Fiber: 5g
- Sugar: 4g
- Sodium: 360mg
- Vitamin A: 30% DV
- Calcium: 15% DV
- Magnesium: 10% DV

Mediterranean Tuna-Stuffed Avocados

 Cooking Time: 0 minutes

 Prep Time: 10 minutes

 Servings: 2

A creamy, flavorful, no-cook lunch packed with heart-healthy fats and protein. This Mediterranean-style twist on tuna salad uses olives, herbs, and lemon juice to brighten the filling, served in nutrient-rich avocado halves. Great for brain health, joint support, and energy regulation.

Ingredients:

- 1 ripe avocado, halved and pit removed
- 1 (5 oz) can tuna in olive oil, drained
- 1 tbsp chopped kalamata olives
- 1 tbsp chopped red onion
- 1 tbsp chopped parsley
- Juice of 1/2 lemon
- Salt and pepper to taste
- Optional: cherry tomatoes or cucumber slices on the side

Instructions:

1. In a small bowl, combine tuna, olives, red onion, parsley, and lemon juice.
2. Mix well and season with salt and pepper to taste.
3. Spoon the tuna mixture evenly into each avocado half.
4. Serve immediately with fresh tomatoes or cucumber slices on the side, if desired.

Nutrition Breakdown (per serving):

- Calories: ~350
- Protein: 18g
- Fat: 26g
- Carbohydrates: 8g
- Fiber: 6g
- Sugar: 1g
- Sodium: 320mg
- Potassium: 20% DV
- Vitamin E: 25% DV
- Omega-3s: 35% DV

CHAPTER 4: LUNCH

Chickpea & Spinach Patties

 Cooking Time: 10 minutes

 Prep Time: 10 minutes

 Servings: 2 (makes about 4 small patties)

These savory, protein-rich patties are made with mashed chickpeas, spinach, and aromatic spices. They're crisp on the outside, tender on the inside, and perfect for a light Mediterranean lunch. High in fiber and antioxidants, they support gut health, joint mobility, and stable energy.

Ingredients:

- 1 cup canned chickpeas, rinsed and mashed
- 1/2 cup chopped fresh spinach
- 1 egg
- 2 tbsp oat flour or breadcrumbs
- 1 clove garlic, minced
- 1/4 tsp ground cumin
- 1/4 tsp smoked paprika (optional)
- Salt and pepper to taste
- 1 tbsp olive oil (for cooking)
- Optional: plain Greek yogurt or tzatziki for serving

Instructions:

1. In a mixing bowl, combine mashed chickpeas, chopped spinach, egg, flour/breadcrumbs, garlic, cumin, paprika, salt, and pepper.
2. Mix until combined. Form into 4 small patties.
3. Heat olive oil in a nonstick skillet over medium heat.
4. Cook patties for about 4-5 minutes per side until golden brown and heated through.
5. Serve warm with a side of Greek yogurt or tzatziki if desired.

Nutrition Breakdown (per serving):

- Calories: ~300
- Protein: 12g
- Fat: 14g
- Carbohydrates: 30g
- Fiber: 7g
- Sugar: 2g
- Sodium: 280mg
- Folate: 35% DV
- Iron: 15% DV
- Vitamin K: 40% DV

Roasted Cauliflower & Lentil Bowl

Cooking Time: 25 minutes
Prep Time: 10 minutes
Servings: 2

This hearty plant-based bowl is packed with flavor and texture—featuring spiced, roasted cauliflower and earthy lentils, all tossed with fresh greens and a creamy lemon-tahini dressing. It's rich in fiber, iron, and anti-inflammatory nutrients, making it ideal for digestion, heart health, and stable energy.

Ingredients:

For the Bowl:
- 2 cups cauliflower florets
- 1 tbsp olive oil
- 1/2 tsp ground cumin
- 1/4 tsp smoked paprika
- Salt and pepper to taste
- 1 cup cooked green or brown lentils
- 1 cup baby arugula or spinach
- 1 tbsp chopped parsley (optional)

For the Dressing:
- 2 tbsp tahini
- Juice of 1/2 lemon
- 1 tbsp water (more as needed)
- Pinch of salt

Instructions:

1. Preheat oven to 400°F (200°C). Line a baking sheet with parchment paper.
2. Toss cauliflower florets with olive oil, cumin, paprika, salt, and pepper. Spread evenly on the baking sheet.
3. Roast for 20–25 minutes, flipping halfway through, until golden and tender.
4. In a small bowl, whisk together tahini, lemon juice, water, and salt until smooth. Adjust consistency as needed.
5. In serving bowls, layer arugula, lentils, and roasted cauliflower.
6. Drizzle with tahini dressing and sprinkle with parsley. Serve warm or at room temperature.

Nutrition Breakdown (per serving):

- Calories: ~340
- Protein: 14g
- Fat: 16g
- Carbohydrates: 35g
- Fiber: 10g
- Sugar: 4g
- Sodium: 200mg
- Iron: 20% DV
- Vitamin C: 60% DV
- Folate: 30% DV

CHAPTER 4: LUNCH

Eggplant & Tomato Stew (Caponata Style)

Cooking Time: 25 minutes

Prep Time: 10 minutes

Servings: 2

This rustic Sicilian-inspired stew is loaded with tender eggplant, juicy tomatoes, onions, and a touch of briny capers. Served warm or at room temperature, it's a fiber-rich, antioxidant-packed lunch that supports blood sugar balance, digestion, and cognitive health—especially great for seniors.

Ingredients:

- 1 medium eggplant, diced
- 1/2 medium onion, chopped
- 1 clove garlic, minced
- 1 cup canned diced tomatoes (with juices)
- 1 tbsp capers (rinsed)
- 1 tbsp olive oil
- 1/2 tsp dried oregano
- Salt and pepper to taste
- Optional: 1 tsp red wine vinegar or a pinch of crushed red pepper flakes
- Optional: fresh basil for garnish

Instructions:

1. Heat olive oil in a large skillet over medium heat.
2. Add chopped onion and cook for 3-4 minutes until translucent.
3. Stir in garlic and cook for 30 seconds more.
4. Add diced eggplant and a pinch of salt. Sauté for 5-7 minutes until starting to soften.
5. Pour in diced tomatoes (with juice), oregano, capers, and optional vinegar or red pepper. Stir well.
6. Cover and simmer for 10-15 minutes, stirring occasionally, until the eggplant is very tender.
7. Season with salt and pepper to taste. Garnish with basil if desired and serve warm or chilled.

Nutrition Breakdown (per serving):

- Calories: ~240
- Protein: 5g
- Fat: 12g
- Carbohydrates: 30g
- Fiber: 9g
- Sugar: 10g
- Sodium: 280mg
- Potassium: 15% DV
- Vitamin A: 10% DV
- Vitamin C: 25% DV

Sardine & Avocado Toast

Cooking Time: 0 minutes
Prep Time: 5 minutes
Servings: 1

This quick and nutrient-dense lunch combines creamy avocado with omega-3-rich sardines on hearty whole grain toast. It's a brain-boosting, heart-healthy, and anti-inflammatory Mediterranean option that's especially supportive for aging adults.

Ingredients:

- 1 slice whole grain or sprouted grain bread
- 1/2 ripe avocado
- 1/2 can sardines in olive oil, drained
- Squeeze of lemon juice
- Pinch of sea salt and black pepper
- Optional: chopped fresh parsley or red chili flakes

Instructions:

1. Toast the slice of bread to your liking.
2. Mash the avocado and spread it evenly over the toast.
3. Top with sardines, breaking them into smaller pieces as needed.
4. Squeeze lemon juice over the top.
5. Season with salt and pepper. Add parsley or chili flakes if desired.
6. Serve immediately.

Nutrition Breakdown (per serving):

- Calories: ~320
- Protein: 18g
- Fat: 22g
- Carbohydrates: 20g
- Fiber: 6g
- Sugar: 1g
- Sodium: 300mg
- Omega-3s: 100% DV
- Vitamin D: 70% DV
- Calcium: 20% DV

CHAPTER 4: LUNCH

Lentil & Feta-Stuffed Sweet Potatoes

 Cooking Time: 30 minutes (for roasting sweet potatoes)

 Prep Time: 10 minutes

 Servings: 2

This cozy and colorful lunch features sweet potatoes roasted to perfection, then stuffed with savory lentils, fresh herbs, and tangy feta. It's high in fiber, iron, and complex carbohydrates—supporting energy, blood sugar regulation, and gut health for older adults.

Ingredients:

- 2 small or medium sweet potatoes
- 1 cup cooked green or brown lentils
- 1/4 cup crumbled feta cheese
- 2 tbsp chopped parsley
- 1 tbsp lemon juice
- 1 tbsp olive oil
- Salt and pepper to taste
- Optional: pinch of ground cumin or paprika

Instructions:

1. Preheat oven to 400°F (200°C). Wash and scrub sweet potatoes, then prick a few times with a fork.
2. Place on a baking sheet and roast for 30-35 minutes, or until tender when pierced with a fork.
3. While the potatoes cook, combine lentils, parsley, lemon juice, olive oil, and optional spices in a bowl. Mix and season to taste.
4. Once the sweet potatoes are done, let cool slightly, then slice open lengthwise and fluff the insides with a fork.
5. Spoon lentil mixture into the center of each potato and top with crumbled feta.
6. Serve warm or at room temperature.

Nutrition Breakdown (per serving):

- Calories: ~370
- Protein: 14g
- Fat: 14g
- Carbohydrates: 45g
- Fiber: 9g
- Sugar: 9g
- Sodium: 280mg
- Iron: 20% DV
- Vitamin A: 250% DV
- Magnesium: 15% DV

MEDITERRANEAN DIET COOKBOOK FOR SENIORS

Chicken Souvlaki Skewers with Tzatziki

 Cooking Time: 12–15 minutes

 Prep Time: 10 minutes (plus optional marinating time)

 Servings: 2

A classic Mediterranean favorite made simple. These tender, herbed chicken skewers are grilled to perfection and served with creamy tzatziki and a side of fresh veggies. Packed with protein and flavor, this lunch supports muscle strength, gut health, and heart wellness.

Ingredients:

For the Chicken Skewers:
- 2 small boneless, skinless chicken breasts, cut into chunks
- 1 tbsp olive oil
- Juice of 1/2 lemon
- 1 tsp dried oregano
- 1/2 tsp garlic powder
- Salt and pepper to taste
- Optional: 1/2 tsp smoked paprika
- 4 small wooden or metal skewers (if wooden, soak in water for 15 min)

For Serving:
- 1/2 cup tzatziki sauce (store-bought or homemade)
- Sliced cucumber, cherry tomatoes, and/or lettuce

Instructions:

1. In a bowl, combine chicken chunks with olive oil, lemon juice, oregano, garlic powder, salt, pepper, and optional paprika. Toss well.
2. Thread the chicken onto skewers.
3. Heat a grill or grill pan over medium-high heat. Cook skewers for about 5–7 minutes per side or until fully cooked and lightly charred.
4. Serve hot with tzatziki and a side of fresh vegetables.

Nutrition Breakdown (per serving):

- Calories: ~360
- Protein: 35g
- Fat: 20g
- Carbohydrates: 8g
- Fiber: 1g
- Sugar: 2g
- Sodium: 300mg
- Vitamin B6: 40% DV
- Zinc: 20% DV
- Calcium: 8% DV

Spinach & Olive Whole Grain Pasta

Cooking Time: 12 minutes
Prep Time: 5 minutes
Servings: 2

A simple, flavorful Mediterranean pasta dish featuring sautéed spinach, briny olives, garlic, and extra virgin olive oil. This quick lunch is rich in fiber, heart-healthy fats, and antioxidants—ideal for supporting digestion and cardiovascular health in older adults.

Ingredients:

- 4 oz whole grain pasta (penne or spaghetti)
- 2 tsp olive oil
- 1 clove garlic, minced
- 2 cups fresh baby spinach
- 1/4 cup chopped kalamata olives
- 1 tbsp grated Parmesan cheese (optional)
- Salt and pepper to taste
- Optional: pinch of crushed red pepper flakes or squeeze of lemon

Instructions:

1. Cook pasta according to package instructions. Drain and set aside.
2. In a large skillet, heat olive oil over medium heat.
3. Add garlic and cook for 30 seconds until fragrant.
4. Add spinach and sauté until wilted, about 2-3 minutes.
5. Stir in cooked pasta and olives. Toss to combine and heat through.
6. Season with salt, pepper, and optional red pepper flakes or lemon.
7. Serve with a sprinkle of Parmesan, if desired.

Nutrition Breakdown (per serving):

- Calories: ~360
- Protein: 12g
- Fat: 14g
- Carbohydrates: 46g
- Fiber: 7g
- Sugar: 3g
- Sodium: 320mg
- Iron: 15% DV
- Magnesium: 20% DV
- Vitamin K: 90% DV

Bulgur Salad with Parsley & Pomegranate

 Cooking Time: 10 minutes (for bulgur)

 Prep Time: 10 minutes

 Servings: 2

This vibrant, tangy grain salad is loaded with fiber, antioxidants, and fresh herbs. Bulgur wheat is tossed with parsley, pomegranate seeds, lemon, and olive oil for a light yet satisfying Mediterranean lunch that supports digestive and cardiovascular health.

Ingredients:

- 1/2 cup dry bulgur wheat
- 1 cup boiling water
- 1/2 cup chopped fresh parsley
- 1/4 cup pomegranate seeds
- 1 small cucumber, diced
- 1 green onion, finely sliced
- Juice of 1 lemon
- 1 tbsp extra virgin olive oil
- Salt and pepper to taste

Instructions:

1. Place bulgur in a heatproof bowl. Pour boiling water over it, cover, and let sit for 10 minutes until tender and fluffy. Fluff with a fork and let cool slightly.
2. Add parsley, pomegranate seeds, cucumber, and green onion to the bulgur.
3. In a small bowl, whisk together lemon juice, olive oil, salt, and pepper.
4. Pour dressing over salad and toss to combine.
5. Chill or serve at room temperature.

Nutrition Breakdown (per serving):

- Calories: ~280
- Protein: 6g
- Fat: 10g
- Carbohydrates: 42g
- Fiber: 8g
- Sugar: 6g
- Sodium: 180mg
- Vitamin C: 25% DV
- Iron: 10% DV
- Folate: 20% DV

CHAPTER 4: LUNCH

Roasted Red Pepper & Hummus Wrap

 Prep Time: 10 minutes

 Cooking Time: 0 minutes

 Servings: 1

This vibrant wrap combines the smoky sweetness of roasted red peppers with creamy hummus, fresh greens, and a light, whole-grain wrap. It's a quick, nutrient-dense meal that's rich in fiber, healthy fats, and antioxidants—perfect for a balanced lunch or snack.

Ingredients:

- 2 whole wheat wraps
- 1/2 cup hummus
- 1/2 cup roasted red peppers (jarred or homemade), sliced
- 1/2 cup baby spinach or mixed greens
- 1/4 cup sliced cucumber
- Optional: a few thin red onion slices or a sprinkle of feta

Instructions:

1. Lay each wrap flat on a plate or cutting board.
2. Spread 1/4 cup hummus evenly over each wrap.
3. Layer roasted red peppers, spinach, cucumber, and any optional extras.
4. Roll up tightly, slice in half if desired, and serve chilled or at room temperature.

Nutrition Breakdown (per serving):

- Calories: ~320
- Protein: 10g
- Fat: 14g
- Carbohydrates: 36g
- Fiber: 7g
- Sugar: 3g
- Sodium: 300mg
- Vitamin A: 35% DV
- Vitamin E: 20% DV
- Iron: 12% DV

Baked Cod with Tomato & Olive Tapenade

 Cooking Time: 15–18 minutes

 Prep Time: 10 minutes

 Servings: 2

This light, Mediterranean-style fish dish features flaky baked cod topped with a savory tomato and olive tapenade. It's rich in lean protein and omega-3s, supporting brain health, inflammation reduction, and cardiovascular function—perfect for seniors seeking a simple, elegant lunch.

Ingredients:

- 2 cod fillets (4–6 oz each)
- 1 tbsp olive oil
- 1/2 tsp dried oregano
- Salt and pepper to taste

For the Tapenade:

- 1/2 cup cherry tomatoes, chopped
- 1/4 cup chopped kalamata olives
- 1 tsp capers (optional)
- 1 clove garlic, minced
- 1 tbsp chopped fresh parsley or basil
- Juice of 1/2 lemon
- 1 tbsp olive oil

Instructions:

1. Preheat oven to 375°F (190°C). Line a baking dish with parchment or lightly grease.
2. Place cod fillets in the dish. Drizzle with olive oil and sprinkle with oregano, salt, and pepper.
3. Bake for 15–18 minutes, or until fish flakes easily with a fork.
4. While cod bakes, combine all tapenade ingredients in a bowl and mix well.
5. Spoon the fresh tapenade over the baked cod before serving.
6. Serve warm with a side of greens or whole grain if desired.

Nutrition Breakdown (per serving):

- Calories: ~330
- Protein: 28g
- Fat: 18g
- Carbohydrates: 8g
- Fiber: 2g
- Sugar: 3g
- Sodium: 340mg
- Omega-3s: 50% DV
- Vitamin D: 70% DV
- Selenium: 80% DV

CHAPTER 5: DINNER

Lemon Herb Baked Chicken Thighs

Cooking Time: 30 minutes
Prep Time: 10 minutes
Servings: 2

Tender, juicy chicken thighs are baked with olive oil, lemon, garlic, and fresh herbs for a classic Mediterranean dinner that's simple and packed with flavor. Served with roasted vegetables or a side salad, this dish supports immune health, muscle strength, and healthy aging.

Ingredients:

- 4 bone-in, skin-on chicken thighs
- 1 1/2 tbsp olive oil
- Juice of 1 lemon
- 2 garlic cloves, minced
- 1 tsp dried oregano (or 1 tbsp chopped fresh)
- 1/2 tsp rosemary (dried or fresh)
- Salt and pepper to taste
- Optional: lemon slices for garnish

Instructions:

1. Preheat oven to 400°F (200°C).
2. Pat chicken thighs dry with a paper towel and place in a baking dish or oven-safe skillet.
3. In a small bowl, whisk together olive oil, lemon juice, garlic, oregano, rosemary, salt, and pepper.
4. Pour the mixture over the chicken and rub to coat evenly.
5. Optional: tuck a few lemon slices between the thighs for extra flavor.
6. Bake uncovered for 30–35 minutes, or until the skin is crispy and the internal temperature reaches 165°F (74°C).
7. Let rest 5 minutes before serving. Serve with a side of roasted vegetables, salad, or whole grain.

Nutrition Breakdown (per serving):

- Calories: ~380
- Protein: 28g
- Fat: 28g
- Carbohydrates: 3g
- Fiber: 0g
- Sugar: 0g
- Sodium: 280mg
- Vitamin B6: 30% DV
- Zinc: 25% DV
- Iron: 10% DV

Baked Eggplant Parmesan (Lightened Up)

 Cooking Time: 25 minutes

 Prep Time: 15 minutes

 Servings: 2

This lighter take on the Italian classic skips the frying in favor of baking, resulting in a tender, flavorful dish that's lower in saturated fat and easier to digest. Eggplant is layered with marinara and mozzarella for a comforting, senior-friendly Mediterranean meal.

Ingredients:

- 1 medium eggplant, sliced into 1/2-inch rounds
- 1/2 tsp salt
- 1/2 cup marinara sauce (low-sodium if possible)
- 1/2 cup shredded part-skim mozzarella cheese
- 2 tbsp grated Parmesan cheese
- 1/4 tsp dried oregano
- 1 tbsp olive oil
- Fresh basil (optional, for garnish)

Instructions:

1. Preheat oven to 400°F (200°C). Line a baking sheet with parchment paper.
2. Sprinkle eggplant slices with salt and let sit for 10 minutes to draw out moisture. Pat dry.
3. Brush both sides of each eggplant slice with olive oil and arrange on the baking sheet.
4. Bake for 15 minutes, flipping halfway through, until lightly golden and tender.
5. In a small baking dish, layer half of the eggplant slices, top with half the marinara, half the mozzarella, and a sprinkle of Parmesan.
6. Repeat the layers, finishing with cheese and oregano.
7. Return to the oven and bake for 10-12 minutes, until bubbly and lightly browned on top.
8. Let cool slightly. Garnish with fresh basil if desired and serve warm.

Nutrition Breakdown (per serving):

- Calories: ~300
- Protein: 13g
- Fat: 18g
- Carbohydrates: 24g
- Fiber: 6g
- Sugar: 8g
- Sodium: 400mg
- Calcium: 20% DV
- Vitamin C: 15% DV
- Potassium: 12% DV

Grilled Sea Bass with Olive Tapenade

 Cooking Time: 10 minutes

 Prep Time: 10 minutes

 Servings: 2

This elegant, heart-healthy dinner features tender grilled sea bass topped with a bold, briny olive tapenade. Packed with omega-3s and Mediterranean flavor, it's light on the stomach and rich in nutrients—perfect for supporting brain health, mood, and inflammation control.

Ingredients:

For the Sea Bass:
- 2 sea bass fillets (5-6 oz each)
- 1 tbsp olive oil
- Juice of 1/2 lemon
- Salt and pepper to taste

For the Olive Tapenade:
- 1/4 cup chopped kalamata olives
- 1 tbsp capers, rinsed
- 1 tbsp chopped fresh parsley
- 1 tsp lemon zest
- 1/2 tbsp olive oil
- Optional: 1 clove garlic, minced (for more bite)

Instructions:

1. Pat sea bass fillets dry and rub with olive oil, lemon juice, salt, and pepper.
2. Heat a grill pan or outdoor grill over medium-high heat.
3. Grill fish for 4-5 minutes per side, or until it flakes easily with a fork. Remove and set aside.
4. In a small bowl, combine all tapenade ingredients. Mix well.
5. Spoon the olive tapenade over the grilled fish and serve immediately.
6. Pair with a side of steamed greens, couscous, or roasted vegetables.

Nutrition Breakdown (per serving):

- Calories: ~360
- Protein: 32g
- Fat: 22g
- Carbohydrates: 4g
- Fiber: 1g
- Sugar: 0g
- Sodium: 400mg
- Omega-3s: 100% DV
- Vitamin D: 80% DV
- Selenium: 70% DV

CHAPTER 5: DINNER

One-Pan Mediterranean Chicken & Veggies

Cooking Time: 30 minutes
Prep Time: 10 minutes
Servings: 2

This one-pan meal is a weeknight staple: juicy chicken, roasted veggies, and Mediterranean herbs all baked together for easy cleanup and balanced nutrition. Full of color, fiber, and flavor, it supports immunity, joint health, and sustained energy—perfect for seniors.

Ingredients:

- 2 boneless, skinless chicken breasts
- 1 small zucchini, chopped
- 1/2 red bell pepper, chopped
- 1/2 red onion, sliced
- 1/2 cup cherry tomatoes
- 1 tbsp olive oil
- Juice of 1/2 lemon
- 1 tsp dried oregano
- 1/4 tsp garlic powder
- Salt and pepper to taste
- Optional: crumbled feta or chopped olives for garnish

Instructions:

1. Preheat oven to 400°F (200°C). Line a baking sheet with parchment or lightly oil a baking dish.
2. Place chicken breasts in the center and surround with chopped zucchini, bell pepper, onion, and tomatoes.
3. In a small bowl, mix olive oil, lemon juice, oregano, garlic powder, salt, and pepper.
4. Drizzle the mixture evenly over chicken and vegetables. Toss veggies gently to coat.
5. Bake for 25-30 minutes, or until chicken is cooked through (165°F internal temperature) and veggies are tender.
6. Garnish with feta or olives, if using. Serve warm.

Nutrition Breakdown (per serving):

- Calories: ~370
- Protein: 34g
- Fat: 18g
- Carbohydrates: 18g
- Fiber: 5g
- Sugar: 6g
- Sodium: 320mg
- Vitamin C: 70% DV
- Potassium: 20% DV
- Iron: 10% DV

Chickpea & Spinach Curry with Brown Rice

 Cooking Time: 20 minutes

 Prep Time: 10 minutes

 Servings: 2

This comforting, plant-based curry is loaded with warming spices, tender chickpeas, and nutrient-rich spinach. Served over hearty brown rice, it's rich in fiber, plant protein, and anti-inflammatory benefits—ideal for seniors looking to support digestion, heart health, and immunity.

Ingredients:

- 1 tbsp olive oil
- 1/2 onion, chopped
- 2 cloves garlic, minced
- 1 tsp ground cumin
- 1/2 tsp ground turmeric
- 1/2 tsp ground coriander
- 1/4 tsp ground cinnamon (optional)
- 1/4 tsp salt
- 1 can (15 oz) chickpeas, drained and rinsed
- 1/2 cup canned diced tomatoes (or crushed)
- 1/3 cup water or low-sodium vegetable broth
- 2 cups fresh spinach, chopped
- 1 cup cooked brown rice (for serving)
- Optional: squeeze of lemon or dollop of yogurt

Instructions:

1. Heat olive oil in a skillet over medium heat. Add onion and sauté for 4-5 minutes until soft.
2. Stir in garlic and all the spices. Cook for 1 minute until fragrant.
3. Add chickpeas, tomatoes, and broth/water. Simmer uncovered for 8-10 minutes.
4. Stir in chopped spinach and cook for another 2 minutes until wilted.
5. Adjust seasoning to taste.
6. Serve curry over warm brown rice. Add lemon juice or a spoonful of yogurt if desired.

Nutrition Breakdown (per serving):

- Calories: ~390
- Protein: 14g
- Fat: 13g
- Carbohydrates: 50g
- Fiber: 11g
- Sugar: 6g
- Sodium: 300mg
- Iron: 25% DV
- Vitamin A: 70% DV
- Magnesium: 20% DV

CHAPTER 5: DINNER

Stuffed Zucchini Boats with Turkey & Feta

 Cooking Time: 25 minutes

 Prep Time: 10 minutes

 Servings: 2

These zucchini boats are a low-carb, high-protein Mediterranean dinner that's big on flavor and gentle on digestion. Lean ground turkey is sautéed with herbs and garlic, then stuffed into roasted zucchini halves and topped with crumbled feta for a satisfying and heart-healthy meal.

Ingredients:

- 2 medium zucchinis, halved lengthwise
- 1/2 lb ground turkey
- 1 clove garlic, minced
- 1/4 cup chopped red onion
- 1/2 tsp dried oregano
- Salt and pepper to taste
- 1/4 cup crumbled feta cheese
- 1 tbsp olive oil
- Optional: fresh parsley or lemon zest for garnish

Instructions:

1. Preheat oven to 400°F (200°C).
2. Scoop out some of the zucchini flesh with a spoon to create "boats," leaving a 1/4-inch shell. Place in a baking dish and brush lightly with olive oil.
3. Roast zucchini halves for 10–12 minutes while you prepare the filling.
4. In a skillet, heat olive oil and sauté red onion for 2–3 minutes.
5. Add garlic and ground turkey. Cook until turkey is browned and cooked through, about 6–8 minutes. Season with oregano, salt, and pepper.
6. Remove zucchini from oven and fill each half with turkey mixture.
7. Top with crumbled feta and return to oven for 8–10 minutes until warmed through and slightly golden.
8. Garnish with fresh parsley or lemon zest if desired. Serve warm.

Nutrition Breakdown (per serving):

- Calories: ~370
- Protein: 28g
- Fat: 22g
- Carbohydrates: 14g
- Fiber: 3g
- Sugar: 5g
- Sodium: 300mg
- Vitamin C: 35% DV
- Calcium: 15% DV
- Iron: 12% DV

Salmon with Lemon-Dill Yogurt Sauce

Cooking Time: 15 minutes

Prep Time: 5 minutes

Servings: 2

A Mediterranean classic, this baked salmon is topped with a creamy lemon-dill yogurt sauce that's light, tangy, and packed with heart-healthy omega-3s. It's easy to digest and supports cognitive health, inflammation reduction, and immune support—an ideal senior-friendly dinner.

Ingredients:

For the Salmon:
- 2 salmon fillets (4-6 oz each)
- 1 tsp olive oil
- Salt and pepper to taste
- Juice of 1/2 lemon

For the Lemon-Dill Yogurt Sauce:
- 1/2 cup plain Greek yogurt
- 1 tbsp fresh dill, chopped (or 1 tsp dried)
- 1 tsp lemon zest
- 1 tbsp lemon juice
- 1/2 garlic clove, minced
- Pinch of salt

Instructions:

1. Preheat oven to 400°F (200°C).
2. Place salmon fillets on a lined baking sheet. Drizzle with olive oil, lemon juice, salt, and pepper.
3. Bake for 12-15 minutes, or until salmon flakes easily with a fork.
4. While the salmon bakes, mix all sauce ingredients in a small bowl until smooth. Adjust seasoning to taste.
5. Plate the salmon and top with a generous spoonful of the yogurt sauce.
6. Serve with steamed greens, roasted vegetables, or quinoa.

Nutrition Breakdown (per serving):

- Calories: ~390
- Protein: 32g
- Fat: 24g
- Carbohydrates: 5g
- Fiber: 0g
- Sugar: 2g
- Sodium: 230mg
- Omega-3s: 80% DV
- Vitamin D: 70% DV
- Calcium: 10% DV

CHAPTER 5: DINNER

Vegetarian Moussaka

 Cooking Time: 35 minutes

 Prep Time: 15 minutes

 Servings: 2

This lighter, plant-based version of the Greek classic layers roasted eggplant with a savory lentil-tomato sauce and creamy yogurt topping. It's rich in fiber, iron, and antioxidants—great for digestion, circulation, and brain health. A deeply satisfying Mediterranean dinner without the heaviness.

Ingredients:

For the Layers:
- 1 medium eggplant, sliced into 1/2-inch rounds
- 1 tbsp olive oil
- Salt and pepper to taste

For the Lentil Filling:
- 1/2 cup cooked green or brown lentils
- 1/2 cup canned diced tomatoes
- 1/4 small onion, finely chopped
- 1 clove garlic, minced
- 1/4 tsp ground cinnamon (optional)
- 1/4 tsp dried oregano
- Salt and pepper to taste

For the Yogurt Topping:
- 1/2 cup plain Greek yogurt
- 1 egg
- 2 tbsp grated Parmesan or crumbled feta
- Pinch of nutmeg (optional)

Instructions:

1. Preheat oven to 375°F (190°C). Brush eggplant slices with olive oil, season, and bake on a parchment-lined tray for 15 minutes, flipping halfway.
2. Meanwhile, sauté onion and garlic in a pan with a touch of olive oil. Add lentils, diced tomatoes, cinnamon, oregano, salt, and pepper. Simmer for 10 minutes until thickened.
3. In a small bowl, whisk together yogurt, egg, cheese, and nutmeg for the topping.
4. In a small baking dish, layer half the eggplant, all the lentil mixture, then the remaining eggplant.
5. Spread the yogurt topping evenly over the top.
6. Bake for 20 minutes or until the top is golden and set. Let rest 5 minutes before serving.

Nutrition Breakdown (per serving):

- Calories: ~400
- Protein: 20g
- Fat: 22g
- Carbohydrates: 30g
- Fiber: 8g
- Sugar: 7g
- Sodium: 320mg
- Iron: 18% DV
- Calcium: 20% DV
- Vitamin A: 15% DV

Greek Lemon Chicken Soup (Avgolemono)

 Cooking Time: 20 minutes

 Prep Time: 10 minutes

 Servings: 2

This comforting Greek classic blends chicken, rice, lemon, and egg into a velvety soup that's light, protein-rich, and easy to digest. It's ideal for immune support, gut health, and a soothing end to the day—especially for seniors seeking warmth and nourishment.

Ingredients:

- 1 small boneless, skinless chicken breast
- 4 cups low-sodium chicken broth
- 1/4 cup uncooked white or brown rice
- 1 egg
- Juice of 1 lemon
- Salt and pepper to taste
- Optional: fresh dill or parsley for garnish

Instructions:

1. In a medium pot, bring the chicken broth to a boil. Add chicken breast and reduce to a simmer. Cook for 12-15 minutes, or until fully cooked. Remove chicken and shred.
2. Add the rice to the broth and simmer for 15-20 minutes (or until tender).
3. In a small bowl, whisk the egg with lemon juice.
4. Slowly ladle about 1/2 cup of hot broth into the egg-lemon mixture while whisking constantly to temper the egg.
5. Slowly pour the tempered egg mixture into the soup pot while stirring gently. Do not boil.
6. Return shredded chicken to the soup, stir, and season with salt and pepper to taste.
7. Serve hot, garnished with dill or parsley if desired.

Nutrition Breakdown (per serving):

- Calories: ~300
- Protein: 25g
- Fat: 10g
- Carbohydrates: 22g
- Fiber: 1g
- Sugar: 1g
- Sodium: 350mg
- Vitamin B12: 20% DV
- Selenium: 35% DV
- Vitamin C: 15% DV

CHAPTER 5: DINNER

Shrimp Saganaki with Tomatoes & Feta

 Cooking Time: 15 minutes

 Prep Time: 10 minutes

 Servings: 2

A quick, classic Greek dish where tender shrimp are simmered in a garlicky tomato sauce and topped with creamy feta. It's rich in protein, calcium, and heart-healthy omega-3s—making it a flavorful, anti-inflammatory meal ideal for senior wellness.

Ingredients:

- 8–10 medium shrimp, peeled and deveined
- 1 tbsp olive oil
- 2 cloves garlic, minced
- 1/4 small onion, finely chopped
- 1 cup canned diced tomatoes (or fresh)
- 1/4 tsp dried oregano
- Salt and pepper to taste
- 1/4 cup crumbled feta cheese
- Optional: fresh parsley or red pepper flakes

Instructions:

1. Heat olive oil in a skillet over medium heat. Add onion and sauté 2–3 minutes until soft.
2. Add garlic and cook for 30 seconds, then pour in the diced tomatoes.
3. Stir in oregano, salt, and pepper. Simmer for 5 minutes to allow flavors to meld.
4. Add shrimp to the pan and cook for 3–4 minutes, flipping halfway, until pink and just cooked through.
5. Sprinkle crumbled feta over the top and cook for 1 more minute to warm the cheese.
6. Garnish with parsley or chili flakes and serve hot, optionally with crusty bread or whole grain.

Nutrition Breakdown (per serving):

- Calories: ~320
- Protein: 28g
- Fat: 18g
- Carbohydrates: 10g
- Fiber: 2g
- Sugar: 4g
- Sodium: 450mg
- Omega-3s: 40% DV
- Calcium: 20% DV
- Vitamin B12: 30% DV

Grilled Lamb Chops with Rosemary & Garlic

 Cooking Time: 10-12 minutes

 Prep Time: 10 minutes (plus optional marinating time)

 Servings: 2

Tender lamb chops seasoned with garlic, rosemary, and olive oil make for a flavorful, nutrient-dense Mediterranean dinner. Rich in protein, iron, and zinc, this dish supports bone health, muscle maintenance, and immune function—great for active aging.

Ingredients:

- 4 small lamb chops (about 3 oz each)
- 1 tbsp olive oil
- 2 garlic cloves, minced
- 1 tsp chopped fresh rosemary (or 1/2 tsp dried)
- Salt and pepper to taste
- Optional: lemon wedges, fresh parsley, or side salad for serving

Instructions:

1. In a small bowl, mix olive oil, garlic, rosemary, salt, and pepper.
2. Rub mixture all over lamb chops. Let marinate for 15-30 minutes (or up to 4 hours in the fridge).
3. Preheat a grill or grill pan over medium-high heat.
4. Grill lamb chops for about 4-5 minutes per side for medium doneness (adjust based on thickness and preference).
5. Let rest for 5 minutes. Serve warm with lemon wedges or a fresh cucumber-tomato salad.

Nutrition Breakdown (per serving):

- Calories: ~420
- Protein: 30g
- Fat: 30g
- Carbohydrates: 1g
- Fiber: 0g
- Sugar: 0g
- Sodium: 180mg
- Iron: 25% DV
- Zinc: 40% DV
- Vitamin B12: 60% DV

CHAPTER 5: DINNER

Stuffed Bell Peppers with Rice & Herbs

 Cooking Time: 30 minutes

 Prep Time: 10 minutes

 Servings: 2

A light, vegetarian Mediterranean dinner filled with fiber, antioxidants, and flavor. These bell peppers are stuffed with brown rice, fresh herbs, pine nuts, and a hint of lemon—great for digestion, heart health, and stable energy, especially for seniors seeking plant-based options.

Ingredients:

- 2 large bell peppers, halved and seeds removed
- 1 cup cooked brown rice
- 2 tbsp chopped fresh parsley
- 1 tbsp chopped fresh mint (or 1/2 tsp dried)
- 1 tbsp pine nuts (optional)
- 1 tbsp olive oil
- Juice of 1/2 lemon
- Salt and pepper to taste
- Optional: 2 tbsp crumbled feta or 1 tbsp raisins for sweetness

Instructions:

1. Preheat oven to 375°F (190°C).
2. In a mixing bowl, combine cooked rice, herbs, pine nuts, olive oil, lemon juice, and salt and pepper. Add feta or raisins if using.
3. Fill each bell pepper half with the rice mixture.
4. Place in a baking dish and cover loosely with foil.
5. Bake for 25-30 minutes, or until peppers are tender.
6. Remove from oven, uncover, and let cool slightly before serving.

Nutrition Breakdown (per serving):

- Calories: ~310
- Protein: 6g
- Fat: 14g
- Carbohydrates: 40g
- Fiber: 6g
- Sugar: 6g
- Sodium: 160mg
- Vitamin C: 150% DV
- Iron: 12% DV
- Magnesium: 15% DV

Baked Tilapia with Herbed Quinoa

 Cooking Time: 15-18 minutes

 Prep Time: 10 minutes

 Servings: 2

This light and nourishing dinner features flaky tilapia fillets seasoned with lemon and herbs, served over fluffy quinoa tossed with parsley and olive oil. High in protein and low in saturated fat, it's an ideal Mediterranean option for heart and brain health.

Ingredients:

For the Tilapia:
- 2 tilapia fillets (4-6 oz each)
- 1 tbsp olive oil
- Juice of 1/2 lemon
- 1/2 tsp dried thyme or oregano
- Salt and pepper to taste

For the Quinoa:
- 1/2 cup dry quinoa (yields ~1½ cups cooked)
- 1 tbsp olive oil
- 2 tbsp chopped fresh parsley
- Juice of 1/2 lemon
- Salt and pepper to taste

Instructions:

1. Preheat oven to 375°F (190°C). Line a baking sheet with parchment or lightly grease it.
2. Place tilapia fillets on the sheet. Drizzle with olive oil and lemon juice, then sprinkle with thyme/oregano, salt, and pepper.
3. Bake for 15-18 minutes, or until the fish flakes easily with a fork.
4. Meanwhile, cook quinoa according to package instructions. Fluff with a fork and stir in olive oil, parsley, lemon juice, salt, and pepper.
5. Plate the fish over the herbed quinoa and serve warm.

Nutrition Breakdown (per serving):

- Calories: ~370
- Protein: 32g
- Fat: 16g
- Carbohydrates: 28g
- Fiber: 4g
- Sugar: 1g
- Sodium: 250mg
- Omega-3s: 30% DV
- Iron: 15% DV
- Magnesium: 20% DV

CHAPTER 5: DINNER

Lentil & Sweet Potato Stew

 Cooking Time: 30 minutes
 Prep Time: 10 minutes
 Servings: 2

A warming and deeply nourishing stew made with protein-rich lentils, sweet potatoes, and Mediterranean spices. This plant-based dinner supports steady energy, blood sugar balance, and digestive health—perfect for seniors looking for comfort food with benefits.

Ingredients:

- 1 tbsp olive oil
- 1/2 onion, chopped
- 1 clove garlic, minced
- 1/2 tsp ground cumin
- 1/4 tsp ground cinnamon
- 1/4 tsp smoked paprika (optional)
- 1 small sweet potato, peeled and diced
- 1/2 cup dry green or brown lentils
- 3 cups low-sodium vegetable broth or water
- 1/2 cup canned diced tomatoes
- Salt and pepper to taste
- Optional: fresh parsley or a squeeze of lemon for serving

Instructions:

1. In a medium pot, heat olive oil over medium heat. Sauté onion for 4-5 minutes until softened.
2. Add garlic, cumin, cinnamon, and paprika. Cook for 30 seconds until fragrant.
3. Stir in sweet potato, lentils, broth, and tomatoes.
4. Bring to a boil, then reduce heat to a simmer. Cover and cook for 25-30 minutes, or until lentils and sweet potatoes are tender.
5. Season with salt and pepper.
6. Serve warm with chopped parsley or a splash of lemon juice if desired.

Nutrition Breakdown (per serving):

- Calories: ~380
- Protein: 16g
- Fat: 10g
- Carbohydrates: 55g
- Fiber: 12g
- Sugar: 9g
- Sodium: 280mg
- Iron: 25% DV
- Vitamin A: 300% DV
- Folate: 60% DV

Cauliflower & Chickpea Tagine

 Cooking Time: 25 minutes

 Prep Time: 10 minutes

 Servings: 2

Inspired by Moroccan flavors, this cozy, spiced stew features tender cauliflower, chickpeas, and warm Mediterranean spices. It's rich in fiber, plant protein, and anti-inflammatory compounds—perfect for supporting joint, gut, and immune health in aging bodies.

Ingredients:

- 1 tbsp olive oil
- 1/2 onion, chopped
- 2 garlic cloves, minced
- 1/2 tsp ground cumin
- 1/2 tsp ground turmeric
- 1/4 tsp ground cinnamon
- 1/4 tsp smoked paprika
- 2 cups cauliflower florets
- 1 cup canned chickpeas, rinsed and drained
- 1/2 cup canned diced tomatoes
- 1/2 cup low-sodium vegetable broth or water
- Salt and pepper to taste
- Optional: 2 tbsp chopped fresh cilantro or parsley, and a squeeze of lemon

Instructions:

1. Heat olive oil in a medium saucepan over medium heat.
2. Add onion and sauté 3-4 minutes until softened. Add garlic and spices and cook 1 minute until fragrant.
3. Stir in cauliflower, chickpeas, tomatoes, and broth. Bring to a simmer.
4. Cover and cook for 20-25 minutes, until the cauliflower is tender and the stew is slightly thickened.
5. Season with salt and pepper.
6. Garnish with fresh herbs and a squeeze of lemon if desired. Serve warm with whole grain couscous or brown rice.

Nutrition Breakdown (per serving):

- Calories: ~360
- Protein: 14g
- Fat: 14g
- Carbohydrates: 45g
- Fiber: 11g
- Sugar: 6g
- Sodium: 260mg
- Vitamin C: 80% DV
- Folate: 45% DV
- Iron: 20% DV

CHAPTER 5: DINNER

Spinach & Feta Stuffed Chicken Breast

 Cooking Time: 25 minutes

 Prep Time: 10 minutes

 Servings: 2

This lean and flavorful dish features tender chicken breasts stuffed with sautéed spinach, garlic, and creamy feta cheese. It's a protein-rich, low-carb Mediterranean dinner that supports muscle health, bone strength, and digestion—perfect for a light, nourishing meal.

Ingredients:

- 2 boneless, skinless chicken breasts
- 1 cup fresh spinach, chopped
- 1 clove garlic, minced
- 1/4 cup crumbled feta cheese
- 1 tbsp olive oil
- Salt and pepper to taste
- Optional: toothpicks or kitchen twine to secure the chicken

Instructions:

1. Preheat oven to 375°F (190°C).
2. Heat 1 tsp of olive oil in a skillet over medium heat. Sauté spinach and garlic for 2–3 minutes until wilted. Remove from heat and let cool slightly.
3. Stir in feta cheese to the spinach mixture.
4. Slice a pocket into the side of each chicken breast (careful not to cut all the way through). Stuff each with half the spinach-feta mixture.
5. Secure with toothpicks or kitchen twine if needed.
6. Rub the outside of each chicken breast with the remaining olive oil and season with salt and pepper.
7. Bake in a lightly oiled baking dish for 25–30 minutes, or until the chicken is cooked through (internal temp of 165°F).
8. Let rest 5 minutes before slicing. Serve warm.

Nutrition Breakdown (per serving):

- Calories: ~370
- Protein: 35g
- Fat: 22g
- Carbohydrates: 4g
- Fiber: 1g
- Sugar: 1g
- Sodium: 310mg
- Calcium: 15% DV
- Vitamin K: 40% DV
- Iron: 12% DV

Mediterranean Vegetable Casserole

 Cooking Time: 35–40 minutes

 Prep Time: 15 minutes

 Servings: 2

A beautiful and nourishing layered dish of zucchini, eggplant, tomatoes, and red onions, baked until tender and flavorful. This plant-based casserole is loaded with fiber, antioxidants, and anti-inflammatory benefits—perfect for digestion, heart health, and overall vitality.

Ingredients:

- 1 small zucchini, thinly sliced
- 1 small eggplant, thinly sliced
- 1 medium tomato, thinly sliced
- 1/2 red onion, thinly sliced
- 1 tbsp olive oil
- 1/2 tsp dried oregano
- 1/4 tsp thyme or basil
- Salt and pepper to taste
- Optional: 1 tbsp grated Parmesan or crumbled feta for topping

Instructions:

1. Preheat oven to 375°F (190°C). Lightly grease a small baking dish.
2. Arrange the sliced vegetables in overlapping layers, alternating zucchini, eggplant, tomato, and onion.
3. Drizzle with olive oil and sprinkle with oregano, thyme (or basil), salt, and pepper.
4. Cover with foil and bake for 25 minutes.
5. Uncover, sprinkle with cheese if using, and bake another 10–15 minutes until veggies are very tender and top is slightly golden.
6. Let rest 5 minutes before serving warm or at room temperature.

Nutrition Breakdown (per serving):

- Calories: ~220
- Protein: 5g
- Fat: 12g
- Carbohydrates: 24g
- Fiber: 7g
- Sugar: 9g
- Sodium: 160mg
- Vitamin C: 70% DV
- Potassium: 15% DV
- Folate: 20% DV

CHAPTER 5: DINNER

Seared Tuna with White Bean Salad

Cooking Time: 6-8 minutes
Prep Time: 10 minutes
Servings: 2

A refreshing, protein-rich Mediterranean dinner featuring seared tuna paired with a lemony white bean salad. This quick and elegant dish is packed with omega-3s, fiber, and antioxidants—ideal for supporting brain health, inflammation control, and heart wellness in older adults.

Ingredients:

For the Tuna:
- 2 ahi tuna steaks (about 4-6 oz each)
- 1 tsp olive oil
- Salt and pepper to taste
- Optional: lemon zest or sesame seeds for garnish

For the White Bean Salad:
- 1 cup canned white beans (like cannellini), rinsed and drained
- 1/2 cup cherry tomatoes, halved
- 1/4 cucumber, diced
- 1 tbsp chopped parsley or basil
- 1 tbsp extra virgin olive oil
- Juice of 1/2 lemon
- Salt and pepper to taste

Instructions:

1. Pat tuna steaks dry and season with salt and pepper.
2. Heat olive oil in a skillet over medium-high heat.
3. Sear tuna for 2-3 minutes per side for medium-rare (or adjust to preferred doneness). Remove and let rest.
4. In a bowl, combine white beans, tomatoes, cucumber, herbs, olive oil, lemon juice, salt, and pepper. Toss gently.
5. Slice tuna and serve alongside or over the salad. Garnish with lemon zest or sesame seeds if desired.

Nutrition Breakdown (per serving):

- Calories: ~400
- Protein: 35g
- Fat: 18g
- Carbohydrates: 22g
- Fiber: 6g
- Sugar: 3g
- Sodium: 250mg
- Omega-3s: 60% DV
- Iron: 20% DV
- Vitamin B12: 70% DV

Quinoa-Stuffed Tomatoes with Basil & Goat Cheese

 Cooking Time: 20 minutes

 Prep Time: 10 minutes

 Servings: 2

These roasted tomatoes are filled with fluffy quinoa, sweet basil, and tangy goat cheese for a bright and balanced Mediterranean dinner. Packed with plant protein, fiber, and antioxidants, they support digestive health, energy, and immunity—especially helpful for seniors looking to eat light and clean.

Ingredients:

- 4 medium tomatoes
- 1/2 cup cooked quinoa
- 2 tbsp goat cheese, crumbled
- 1 tbsp chopped fresh basil
- 1 tbsp chopped parsley (optional)
- 1 tbsp olive oil
- Salt and pepper to taste
- Optional: sprinkle of whole grain breadcrumbs or pine nuts

Instructions:

1. Preheat oven to 375°F (190°C).
2. Cut the tops off the tomatoes and gently scoop out the seeds and pulp. Set aside the hollowed-out shells.
3. In a bowl, mix cooked quinoa with goat cheese, basil, parsley, olive oil, salt, and pepper. Add breadcrumbs or pine nuts if using.
4. Stuff the quinoa mixture into each tomato, gently packing it down.
5. Place in a small baking dish and bake for 18-20 minutes, until tomatoes are soft but still hold their shape.
6. Let cool slightly and serve warm or room temperature.

Nutrition Breakdown (per serving):

- Calories: ~280
- Protein: 9g
- Fat: 15g
- Carbohydrates: 24g
- Fiber: 5g
- Sugar: 6g
- Sodium: 180mg
- Vitamin C: 50% DV
- Folate: 20% DV
- Calcium: 10% DV

CHAPTER 5: DINNER

Roasted Chicken Drumsticks with Garlic & Paprika

Cooking Time: 35–40 minutes

Prep Time: 10 minutes

Servings: 2

This flavorful one-pan dinner features crispy, golden roasted drumsticks seasoned with garlic and smoky paprika. Easy to prepare and budget-friendly, it delivers high-quality protein and minerals to support muscle maintenance and bone health for older adults.

Ingredients:

- 4 skin-on chicken drumsticks
- 1 tbsp olive oil
- 2 cloves garlic, minced
- 1 tsp smoked paprika
- 1/2 tsp dried oregano
- Salt and pepper to taste
- Optional: lemon wedges or chopped parsley for serving

Instructions:

1. Preheat oven to 400°F (200°C). Line a baking sheet with parchment or lightly oil it.
2. In a small bowl, mix olive oil, garlic, paprika, oregano, salt, and pepper.
3. Pat drumsticks dry with a paper towel and rub the seasoning mixture all over the chicken.
4. Arrange on the baking sheet, spaced apart.
5. Roast for 35–40 minutes, flipping halfway through, until skin is crisp and the internal temperature reaches 165°F (74°C).
6. Let rest 5 minutes before serving. Garnish with parsley or lemon if desired.

Nutrition Breakdown (per serving):

- Calories: ~400
- Protein: 30g
- Fat: 28g
- Carbohydrates: 2g
- Fiber: 0g
- Sugar: 0g
- Sodium: 280mg
- Vitamin B6: 30% DV
- Zinc: 25% DV
- Selenium: 40% DV

Eggplant & Lentil Ragu over Whole Wheat Pasta

Cooking Time: 25 minutes
Prep Time: 10 minutes
Servings: 2

This hearty vegetarian twist on Italian ragu features tender eggplant and protein-rich lentils simmered in a savory tomato sauce, served over whole wheat pasta. Packed with fiber, antioxidants, and plant-based iron, it's a nourishing meal that supports energy, digestion, and cardiovascular health.

Ingredients:

- 1 tbsp olive oil
- 1/2 medium eggplant, diced
- 1/2 small onion, chopped
- 2 cloves garlic, minced
- 1/2 cup canned lentils (or 1/4 cup cooked)
- 3/4 cup canned crushed tomatoes
- 1/2 tsp dried oregano
- 1/4 tsp red pepper flakes (optional)
- Salt and pepper to taste
- 4 oz whole wheat pasta (uncooked weight)
- Optional: chopped fresh basil or grated Parmesan

Instructions:

1. Cook pasta according to package directions. Drain and set aside.
2. In a large skillet, heat olive oil over medium heat. Add onion and sauté for 2-3 minutes.
3. Add eggplant and a pinch of salt. Cook for 6-8 minutes, stirring occasionally, until soft.
4. Stir in garlic, lentils, crushed tomatoes, oregano, and red pepper flakes (if using).
5. Simmer for 10-12 minutes, allowing the sauce to thicken slightly. Adjust seasoning as needed.
6. Toss the ragu with cooked pasta and top with basil or Parmesan if desired. Serve warm.

Nutrition Breakdown (per serving):

- Calories: ~390
- Protein: 15g
- Fat: 14g
- Carbohydrates: 50g
- Fiber: 10g
- Sugar: 9g
- Sodium: 280mg
- Iron: 20% DV
- Magnesium: 15% DV
- Vitamin C: 25% DV

CHAPTER 5: DINNER

Zucchini Noodle Stir-Fry with Tofu

 Cooking Time: 10 minutes

 Prep Time: 10 minutes

 Servings: 2

This light, quick stir-fry swaps traditional noodles for spiralized zucchini, tossed with golden tofu, bell peppers, and garlic. It's low-carb, rich in plant protein, and full of antioxidants—perfect for seniors looking for a flavorful, digestion-friendly Mediterranean-style dinner.

Ingredients:

- 2 medium zucchinis, spiralized
- 1/2 block firm tofu (about 7 oz), cubed
- 1 tbsp olive oil (or avocado oil)
- 1/2 red bell pepper, thinly sliced
- 1 garlic clove, minced
- 1 tbsp low-sodium tamari or soy sauce
- 1/2 tsp sesame seeds (optional)
- Salt and pepper to taste
- Optional: chopped fresh basil or parsley

Instructions:

1. Pat tofu dry and cut into cubes.
2. Heat half of the oil in a nonstick skillet over medium heat. Add tofu and cook until golden and crisp on most sides, about 6-8 minutes. Remove and set aside.
3. In the same pan, add the remaining oil and sauté bell pepper and garlic for 1-2 minutes.
4. Add zucchini noodles and cook another 2-3 minutes, just until tender.
5. Return tofu to the pan and add tamari. Toss everything gently to combine.
6. Sprinkle with sesame seeds and herbs if desired. Serve immediately.

Nutrition Breakdown (per serving):

- Calories: ~320
- Protein: 16g
- Fat: 20g
- Carbohydrates: 16g
- Fiber: 4g
- Sugar: 5g
- Sodium: 300mg
- Calcium: 20% DV
- Iron: 15% DV
- Magnesium: 12% DV

97

White Fish en Papillote with Lemon & Herbs

 Cooking Time: 15-18 minutes

 Prep Time: 10 minutes

 Servings: 2

This elegant Mediterranean-style dinner involves gently baking white fish (like cod or halibut) in parchment paper with lemon, olive oil, and fresh herbs. The result is a moist, flavorful, and heart-healthy meal that's easy to digest and perfect for seniors looking for light, nourishing protein.

Ingredients:

- 2 white fish fillets (cod, haddock, or halibut - about 5 oz each)
- 1 tbsp olive oil
- 1/2 lemon, thinly sliced
- 1 tbsp chopped fresh parsley or dill
- Salt and pepper to taste
- Optional: 4-6 cherry tomatoes or a few sliced zucchini rounds
- 2 sheets of parchment paper or foil

Instructions:

1. Preheat oven to 375°F (190°C).
2. Place each fish fillet in the center of a parchment sheet. Drizzle with olive oil and sprinkle with salt, pepper, and fresh herbs.
3. Top each fillet with 2-3 lemon slices and optional vegetables if using.
4. Fold the parchment into a sealed packet (like a pouch), tucking the edges under to trap steam.
5. Place packets on a baking sheet and bake for 15-18 minutes, or until the fish flakes easily with a fork.
6. Carefully open packets to release steam. Serve directly in the paper or transfer to plates.

Nutrition Breakdown (per serving):

- Calories: ~300
- Protein: 30g
- Fat: 16g
- Carbohydrates: 5g
- Fiber: 1g
- Sugar: 1g
- Sodium: 220mg
- Omega-3s: 50% DV
- Vitamin D: 80% DV
- Selenium: 60% DV

CHAPTER 5: DINNER

Stuffed Portobello Mushrooms with Couscous

 Cooking Time: 20 minutes

 Prep Time: 10 minutes

 Servings: 2

These hearty, meaty portobello mushrooms are filled with herbed couscous, sun-dried tomatoes, olives, and a touch of feta. Full of flavor and Mediterranean goodness, this dish is high in fiber, antioxidants, and plant-based nutrients—ideal for seniors looking for a satisfying vegetarian dinner.

Ingredients:

- 2 large portobello mushroom caps, stems removed
- 1/2 cup cooked couscous
- 2 tbsp chopped sun-dried tomatoes (in oil, drained)
- 2 tbsp chopped kalamata olives
- 2 tbsp crumbled feta cheese
- 1 tbsp chopped fresh parsley
- 1 tbsp olive oil
- Salt and pepper to taste
- Optional: 1 clove garlic, minced

Instructions:

1. Preheat oven to 375°F (190°C). Line a baking sheet with parchment.
2. Brush mushroom caps with olive oil and place gill-side up on the baking sheet.
3. In a bowl, combine cooked couscous, sun-dried tomatoes, olives, feta, parsley, and optional garlic. Season with salt and pepper.
4. Spoon the couscous mixture into each mushroom cap, gently pressing to pack it in.
5. Bake for 18-20 minutes, until mushrooms are tender and the tops are lightly golden.
6. Serve warm, optionally garnished with more fresh herbs.

Nutrition Breakdown (per serving):

- Calories: ~340
- Protein: 9g
- Fat: 20g
- Carbohydrates: 32g
- Fiber: 5g
- Sugar: 5g
- Sodium: 350mg
- Iron: 15% DV
- Vitamin B2 (Riboflavin): 30% DV
- Selenium: 20% DV

Chard & Cannellini Bean Sauté

 Cooking Time: 10–12 minutes

 Prep Time: 5 minutes

 Servings: 2

A quick and nourishing Mediterranean side or light main dish, this sauté pairs tender Swiss chard with creamy white beans, garlic, and olive oil. It's rich in fiber, plant-based protein, and minerals—perfect for seniors seeking a digestion-friendly, anti-inflammatory meal.

Ingredients:

- 1 tbsp olive oil
- 1 clove garlic, minced
- 1 bunch Swiss chard, stems removed and leaves chopped
- 1 cup canned cannellini beans, rinsed and drained
- Juice of 1/2 lemon
- Salt and pepper to taste
- Optional: pinch of red pepper flakes or grated Parmesan

Instructions:

1. In a large skillet, heat olive oil over medium heat. Add garlic and sauté for 30 seconds until fragrant.
2. Add chopped Swiss chard and cook, stirring, until wilted—about 3–4 minutes.
3. Stir in cannellini beans and cook another 3–4 minutes, until heated through and well combined.
4. Add lemon juice, salt, and pepper to taste.
5. Sprinkle with red pepper flakes or Parmesan if desired. Serve warm.

Nutrition Breakdown (per serving):

- Calories: ~280
- Protein: 10g
- Fat: 14g
- Carbohydrates: 28g
- Fiber: 8g
- Sugar: 2g
- Sodium: 260mg
- Iron: 20% DV
- Calcium: 15% DV
- Vitamin K: 200% DV

CHAPTER 6: DESSERTS

Greek Yogurt with Honey & Walnuts

 Prep Time: 5 minutes

 Cooking Time: 0 minutes

 Servings: 2

This no-cook dessert is rich in protein, healthy fats, and probiotics. Creamy Greek yogurt pairs perfectly with heart-healthy walnuts and a light drizzle of honey for a naturally sweet and satisfying finish. Great for digestion, brain health, and balanced blood sugar.

Ingredients:

- 1 cup plain Greek yogurt (full-fat or low-fat)
- 2 tbsp chopped walnuts (raw or lightly toasted)
- 2 tsp raw honey (or less, to taste)
- Optional: pinch of cinnamon or a few fresh berries

Instructions:

1. Spoon the Greek yogurt evenly into two small bowls.
2. Top each with 1 tablespoon of chopped walnuts.
3. Drizzle 1 teaspoon of honey over each serving.
4. Add a sprinkle of cinnamon or a few berries, if desired.
5. Serve immediately and enjoy chilled.

Nutrition Breakdown (per serving):

- Calories: ~200
- Protein: 11g
- Fat: 11g
- Carbohydrates: 15g
- Fiber: 1g
- Sugar: 9g (mostly natural)
- Calcium: 15% DV
- Omega-3s: High
- Probiotics: Present

CHAPTER 6: DESSERTS

Olive Oil Citrus Cake (Naturally Sweetened)

Prep Time: 10 minutes
Cooking Time: 30-35 minutes
Servings: 8 small slices

This Mediterranean-style cake is light, moist, and delicately sweetened with maple syrup instead of refined sugar. Made with heart-healthy olive oil and fresh citrus zest, it's perfect for a guilt-free treat that supports energy and inflammation balance.

Ingredients:

- 1 cup almond flour
- 1/2 cup whole wheat flour (or oat flour for gluten-free)
- 1/2 tsp baking powder
- 1/4 tsp baking soda
- 1/4 tsp sea salt
- 1/3 cup extra virgin olive oil
- 1/3 cup maple syrup (or raw honey)
- 2 eggs
- Zest of 1 orange
- Juice of 1/2 orange
- 1 tsp vanilla extract
- Optional: sliced almonds or orange zest for garnish

Instructions:

1. Preheat oven to 350°F (175°C). Lightly oil or line a small 8" loaf pan or cake pan with parchment.
2. In a large bowl, whisk together almond flour, whole wheat flour, baking powder, baking soda, and salt.
3. In another bowl, whisk together olive oil, maple syrup, eggs, orange zest and juice, and vanilla.
4. Pour the wet mixture into the dry and stir until just combined. Do not overmix.
5. Pour the batter into the prepared pan and smooth the top. Sprinkle with sliced almonds or extra zest if desired.
6. Bake for 30-35 minutes, or until a toothpick inserted in the center comes out clean.
7. Let cool completely before slicing. Store covered at room temp for up to 3 days.

Nutrition Breakdown (per slice):

- Calories: ~210
- Protein: 5g
- Fat: 14g
- Carbohydrates: 18g
- Fiber: 2g
- Sugar: 7g (no refined sugar)
- Vitamin E: 15% DV
- Magnesium: 10% DV

Fig & Almond Energy Bites

Prep Time: 10 minutes

Chill Time: 15 minutes

Servings: 12 small bites

These no-bake, naturally sweetened bites are made with fiber-rich dried figs, heart-healthy almonds, and a touch of cinnamon. They're perfect as a healthy Mediterranean-style dessert or a mid-day energy boost—with no added sugar and plenty of nutrients for active aging.

Ingredients:

- 1 cup dried figs (stems removed)
- 1/2 cup raw almonds
- 1/4 cup rolled oats (gluten-free if needed)
- 1 tbsp ground flaxseed or chia seeds (optional)
- 1/2 tsp cinnamon
- 1/2 tsp vanilla extract
- Pinch of sea salt
- 1–2 tbsp warm water, as needed

Instructions:

1. Add figs, almonds, oats, flaxseed, cinnamon, vanilla, and salt to a food processor.
2. Pulse until the mixture is finely chopped and sticky.
3. If the mixture is too dry, add warm water 1 tablespoon at a time and pulse again.
4. Scoop out heaping teaspoons and roll into small balls.
5. Place on a plate and chill in the fridge for 15–20 minutes to firm up.
6. Store and cool in an airtight container for up to 1 week in the refrigerator.

Nutrition Breakdown (per bite):

- Calories: ~90
- Protein: 2g
- Fat: 5g
- Carbohydrates: 9g
- Fiber: 2g
- Sugar: 6g (from figs only)
- Magnesium: 10% DV
- Iron: 6% DV
- Omega-3s: Present (if using flax or chia)

CHAPTER 6: DESSERTS

Lemon Yogurt Mousse with Olive Oil

 Prep Time: 10 minutes

 Chill Time: 30 minutes

 Servings: 2

This airy, tangy mousse is made with protein-rich Greek yogurt, fresh lemon, and a swirl of extra virgin olive oil. It's naturally sweetened with honey (or maple syrup) and offers a creamy, refreshing dessert with heart-healthy fats and probiotics—perfect for a light Mediterranean finish.

Ingredients:

- 3/4 cup plain Greek yogurt (full-fat or low-fat)
- 1 egg white (pasteurized or whipped aquafaba for egg-free option)
- 1 1/2 tbsp raw honey or pure maple syrup
- Zest of 1 lemon
- 1 tbsp fresh lemon juice
- 1 tbsp extra virgin olive oil
- Pinch of salt
- Optional: mint leaves or crushed pistachios for topping

Instructions:

1. In a small bowl, whisk the egg white (or aquafaba) until soft peaks form. Set aside.
2. In another bowl, whisk together the yogurt, honey, lemon zest, lemon juice, olive oil, and a pinch of salt until smooth and fluffy.
3. Gently fold the whipped egg white into the yogurt mixture until just combined.
4. Spoon into small serving glasses or bowls.
5. Chill in the refrigerator for at least 30 minutes.
6. Garnish with mint or pistachios just before serving.

Nutrition Breakdown (per serving):

- Calories: ~180
- Protein: 9g
- Fat: 10g
- Carbohydrates: 15g
- Fiber: 0g
- Sugar: 11g (natural)
- Calcium: 12% DV
- Vitamin C: 10% DV
- Omega-9s: High

Baked Pears with Cinnamon & Walnuts

 Prep Time: 5 minutes

 Cooking Time: 25 minutes

 Servings: 2

Warm, naturally sweet, and full of fiber—this Mediterranean-inspired dessert features ripe pears baked with cinnamon, heart-healthy walnuts, and a touch of olive oil. It's a comforting, low-sugar option that supports digestion, heart health, and blood sugar balance.

Ingredients:

- 2 ripe pears, halved and cored
- 1/4 cup chopped walnuts
- 1/2 tsp ground cinnamon
- 1 tsp extra virgin olive oil
- Optional: drizzle of raw honey (1/2 tsp per pear half)
- Optional topping: a spoonful of Greek yogurt or ricotta

Instructions:

1. Preheat oven to 375°F (190°C).
2. Place pear halves in a small baking dish, cut side up.
3. In a small bowl, toss chopped walnuts with cinnamon and olive oil.
4. Spoon the walnut mixture into the center of each pear half.
5. Bake for 20-25 minutes, or until pears are soft and lightly golden.
6. Drizzle with a touch of honey if using, and serve warm—optionally topped with a spoonful of Greek yogurt or ricotta.

Nutrition Breakdown (per serving – 2 halves):

- Calories: ~210
- Protein: 3g
- Fat: 12g
- Carbohydrates: 26g
- Fiber: 5g
- Sugar: 14g (mostly natural)
- Potassium: 10% DV
- Omega-3s: Present
- Vitamin C: 12% DV

CHAPTER 6: DESSERTS

Tahini Bliss Balls with Dates & Sesame Seeds

Prep Time: 10 minutes

Chill Time: 15-20 minutes

Servings: 12 small balls

These no-bake Mediterranean treats are rich, nutty, and naturally sweetened with fiber-rich dates. Tahini adds a creamy texture and healthy fats, while sesame seeds provide crunch and calcium. A great make-ahead dessert or snack with no refined sugar.

Ingredients:

- 1/2 cup tahini (sesame paste)
- 1/2 cup soft Medjool dates (about 6), pitted
- 1/4 cup almond flour or ground oats
- 1/2 tsp cinnamon
- 1/2 tsp vanilla extract
- Pinch of salt
- 2 tbsp sesame seeds (for rolling)

Instructions:

1. In a food processor, combine tahini, dates, almond flour, cinnamon, vanilla, and salt.
2. Pulse until a thick, sticky dough forms. If it's too dry, add 1 tsp of water at a time until it holds together.
3. Scoop out heaping teaspoons and roll into balls.
4. Roll each ball in sesame seeds to coat.
5. Chill in the fridge for 15-20 minutes to firm up. Store in an airtight container in the refrigerator for up to 1 week.

Nutrition Breakdown (per ball):

- Calories: ~90
- Protein: 2g
- Fat: 6g
- Carbohydrates: 7g
- Fiber: 1.5g
- Sugar: 5g (natural)
- Calcium: 8% DV
- Iron: 6% DV
- Magnesium: 10% DV

Orange & Almond Flour Cookies

 Prep Time: 10 minutes

 Cooking Time: 12-14 minutes

 Servings: 10 small cookies

These soft, naturally gluten-free cookies are made with almond flour, orange zest, and just a touch of maple syrup. Light, chewy, and subtly sweet, they're rich in healthy fats and vitamin E—perfect for a wholesome Mediterranean dessert that supports energy and blood sugar balance.

Ingredients:

- 1 1/2 cups almond flour
- Zest of 1 orange
- 1/4 tsp baking soda
- 1/8 tsp sea salt
- 1/4 tsp ground cinnamon (optional)
- 1 egg
- 2 tbsp olive oil
- 2 tbsp maple syrup (or raw honey)
- 1/2 tsp vanilla extract
- Optional: slivered almonds or extra orange zest for topping

Instructions:

1. Preheat oven to 350°F (175°C). Line a baking sheet with parchment paper.
2. In a bowl, whisk together almond flour, orange zest, baking soda, salt, and cinnamon.
3. In another bowl, whisk egg, olive oil, maple syrup, and vanilla until smooth.
4. Add wet ingredients to the dry and stir to form a soft dough.
5. Scoop tablespoons of dough onto the baking sheet and flatten slightly. Top with almonds or zest if using.
6. Bake for 12-14 minutes, or until edges are golden. Let cool before serving.

Nutrition Breakdown (per cookie):

- Calories: ~120
- Protein: 3g
- Fat: 9g
- Carbohydrates: 7g
- Fiber: 1g
- Sugar: 4g (low)
- Vitamin E: 20% DV
- Magnesium: 10% DV
- Gluten-Free: Yes

CHAPTER 6: DESSERTS

Ricotta with Berries & Balsamic Glaze

Prep Time: 5 minutes

Cooking Time: 0 minutes (or 5 minutes for optional glaze reduction)

Servings: 2

This elegant, no-bake dessert pairs creamy ricotta with antioxidant-rich berries and a tangy balsamic drizzle. It's low in sugar, high in calcium, and beautifully balanced—perfect for seniors wanting a light, nutritious Mediterranean-style treat.

Ingredients:

- 1/2 cup whole milk ricotta cheese
- 1/2 cup mixed fresh berries (strawberries, blueberries, raspberries)
- 2 tsp balsamic glaze (store-bought or homemade)
- Optional: 1/2 tsp honey or maple syrup for extra sweetness
- Optional garnish: fresh mint or crushed pistachios

Instructions:

1. Divide the ricotta into two small bowls or ramekins.
2. Top each with 1/4 cup of fresh berries.
3. Drizzle 1 teaspoon of balsamic glaze over each serving.
4. Add a tiny drizzle of honey or maple syrup if desired.
5. Garnish with fresh mint or pistachios, and serve immediately.

Optional Homemade Balsamic Glaze:

Simmer 1/4 cup balsamic vinegar over low heat until reduced by half and thickened (about 5 minutes). Cool before using.

Nutrition Breakdown (per serving):

- Calories: ~150
- Protein: 6g
- Fat: 8g
- Carbohydrates: 11g
- Fiber: 2g
- Sugar: 6g (mostly natural)
- Calcium: 15% DV
- Vitamin C: 25% DV
- Antioxidants: High

Spiced Poached Apples in Herbal Tea

Prep Time: 5 minutes

Cooking Time: 20 minutes

Servings: 2

This soothing, naturally sweet dessert features apples gently poached in spiced herbal tea with cinnamon, cloves, and orange zest. It's free of added sugar and full of flavor—perfect for calming digestion, supporting immunity, and enjoying a warm, senior-friendly Mediterranean treat.

Ingredients:

- 2 small apples (such as Gala or Honeycrisp), peeled and halved
- 1 1/2 cups brewed herbal tea (hibiscus, rooibos, or chamomile work beautifully)
- 1 strip of orange zest
- 1 cinnamon stick
- 2 whole cloves (or pinch of ground cloves)
- Optional: 1/2 tsp vanilla extract or a splash of lemon juice
- Optional topping: dollop of plain Greek yogurt or crushed walnuts

Instructions:

1. In a small saucepan, combine brewed tea, orange zest, cinnamon stick, cloves, and optional vanilla. Bring to a gentle simmer.
2. Add the halved apples, cut side down, and simmer for 15–20 minutes, or until tender when pierced with a fork.
3. Carefully remove apples and let cool slightly.
4. Serve warm in a small dish with a spoonful of the poaching liquid. Add yogurt or walnuts if desired.

Nutrition Breakdown (per serving):

- Calories: ~100
- Protein: 1g
- Fat: 1g
- Carbohydrates: 24g
- Fiber: 4g
- Sugar: 16g (all natural)
- Vitamin C: 10% DV
- Potassium: 6% DV
- Caffeine-Free: Yes

CHAPTER 6: DESSERTS

Coconut Date Rolls

 Prep Time: 10 minutes

 Chill Time: 15 minutes

 Servings: 10 small rolls

These naturally sweet Mediterranean treats are made with soft Medjool dates, shredded coconut, and optional almonds or sesame seeds. No added sugar, no baking—just fiber, minerals, and satisfying flavor in every bite. A perfect low-sugar dessert or snack for seniors.

Ingredients:

- 1 cup pitted Medjool dates (about 10-12)
- 1/3 cup unsweetened shredded coconut (plus extra for rolling)
- 1/4 cup raw almonds (or walnuts, optional)
- 1/2 tsp vanilla extract
- Pinch of sea salt
- Optional: 1 tbsp sesame seeds or chia seeds

Instructions:

1. In a food processor, combine dates, coconut, almonds, vanilla, and salt.
2. Blend until the mixture becomes sticky and forms a dough-like consistency.
3. Scoop out small portions and roll into balls or short log shapes.
4. Roll each in additional shredded coconut or sesame seeds.
5. Chill in the fridge for 15-20 minutes before serving. Store refrigerated for up to 1 week.

Nutrition Breakdown (per roll):

- Calories: ~90
- Protein: 1.5g
- Fat: 4g
- Carbohydrates: 13g
- Fiber: 2g
- Sugar: 10g (natural)
- Magnesium: 8% DV
- Potassium: 6% DV
- Gluten-Free: Yes

Mini Greek Yogurt Cheesecakes (No-Bake)

Prep Time: 10 minutes

Chill Time: 2 hours

Servings: 4 mini cheesecakes

These creamy, no-bake cheesecakes are made with Greek yogurt, a hint of honey, and a simple almond meal crust. They're naturally sweetened, protein-rich, and perfectly portioned—an elegant Mediterranean-style dessert that's both gut-friendly and indulgent without being heavy.

Ingredients:

For the crust:
- 1/2 cup almond meal or finely ground oats
- 1 tbsp melted coconut oil or olive oil
- 1/2 tsp cinnamon
- Pinch of salt

For the filling:
- 1/2 cup plain Greek yogurt (full-fat or 2%)
- 3 oz cream cheese (softened)
- 1 1/2 tbsp raw honey or maple syrup
- 1/2 tsp vanilla extract
- Optional toppings: fresh berries, sliced figs, or a drizzle of honey

Instructions:

1. In a bowl, mix almond meal, melted oil, cinnamon, and salt until combined.
2. Press the mixture firmly into the bottom of 4 silicone muffin cups or small ramekins.
3. In another bowl, beat together Greek yogurt, cream cheese, honey, and vanilla until smooth and creamy.
4. Spoon the filling evenly over each crust.
5. Chill in the refrigerator for at least 2 hours until set.
6. Top with berries, figs, or a light drizzle of honey before serving.

Nutrition Breakdown (per mini cheesecake):

- Calories: ~180
- Protein: 6g
- Fat: 12g
- Carbohydrates: 12g
- Fiber: 1g
- Sugar: 7g (natural)
- Calcium: 10% DV
- Probiotics: Present
- Gluten-Free: Yes

CHAPTER 6: DESSERTS

Rosewater Pistachio Bites

Prep Time: 10 minutes

Chill Time: 15–20 minutes

Servings: 10 small bites

These delicate no-bake bites combine sweet dates, nutty pistachios, and a hint of floral rosewater for an elegant, naturally sweet Mediterranean dessert. They're rich in fiber, healthy fats, and antioxidants—ideal for a heart-healthy treat with a sophisticated twist.

Ingredients:

- 1/2 cup shelled pistachios (plus extra for rolling)
- 1/2 cup soft Medjool dates, pitted
- 1/4 cup unsweetened shredded coconut
- 1/2 tsp rosewater (use sparingly—it's strong!)
- 1/2 tsp vanilla extract
- Pinch of sea salt
- Optional: 1 tsp orange zest

Instructions:

1. Add pistachios, dates, coconut, rosewater, vanilla, salt, and orange zest (if using) to a food processor.
2. Pulse until the mixture is sticky and forms a dough.
3. Scoop out small portions and roll into balls.
4. Roll in crushed pistachios or coconut to coat.
5. Chill for 15–20 minutes to firm up before serving. Store in an airtight container in the refrigerator for up to 1 week.

Nutrition Breakdown (per bite):

- Calories: ~90
- Protein: 2g
- Fat: 5g
- Carbohydrates: 9g
- Fiber: 1.5g
- Sugar: 6g (natural)
- Magnesium: 10% DV
- Vitamin B6: 6% DV
- Gluten-Free: Yes

Chia Pudding with Almond Milk & Figs

 Prep Time: 5 minutes

 Chill Time: 4+ hours (or overnight)

 Servings: 2

This creamy, no-cook Mediterranean-style pudding is made with almond milk, chia seeds, and naturally sweet figs. It's rich in fiber, omega-3s, and calcium—making it an ideal low-sugar dessert or nourishing snack for seniors.

Ingredients:

- 1 1/2 cups unsweetened almond milk
- 1/4 cup chia seeds
- 1/2 tsp vanilla extract
- 1-2 soft dried figs, finely chopped (or use fresh if available)
- 1 tsp maple syrup or honey (optional, for extra sweetness)
- Optional toppings: sliced almonds, cinnamon, or more chopped figs

Instructions:

1. In a mixing bowl or jar, whisk together almond milk, chia seeds, vanilla, and optional maple syrup.
2. Stir in chopped figs.
3. Cover and refrigerate for at least 4 hours or overnight, stirring once after 30 minutes to prevent clumping.
4. When ready to serve, stir well and spoon into two bowls or jars.
5. Top with additional figs, sliced almonds, or a sprinkle of cinnamon if desired.

Nutrition Breakdown (per serving):

- Calories: ~190
- Protein: 5g
- Fat: 9g
- Carbohydrates: 21g
- Fiber: 9g
- Sugar: 8g (mostly natural)
- Omega-3s: High
- Calcium: 15% DV
- Iron: 10% DV

CHAPTER 6: DESSERTS

Baked Medjool Dates Stuffed with Almond Butter

Prep Time: 5 minutes

Cooking Time: 8-10 minutes (optional, for warm version)

Servings: 6 stuffed dates

This simple Mediterranean dessert is naturally sweet, satisfying, and packed with potassium, magnesium, and healthy fats. Soft Medjool dates are filled with creamy almond butter and gently warmed for a caramel-like finish. It's perfect for a no-fuss, energy-boosting treat.

Ingredients:

- 6 Medjool dates, pitted
- 3 tbsp almond butter (smooth or crunchy)
- Optional toppings:
    - Pinch of sea salt
    - Chopped pistachios or walnuts
    - Shredded coconut
    - Drizzle of dark chocolate (85%+ cacao)

Instructions:

1. Slice each date lengthwise to open, but don't cut all the way through.
2. Fill each date with about 1/2 tablespoon of almond butter.
3. Optional: top with chopped nuts, sea salt, or a sprinkle of coconut.
4. For a warm version, place stuffed dates on a baking tray and bake at 350°F (175°C) for 8-10 minutes until soft and gooey.
5. Serve warm or at room temperature.

Nutrition Breakdown (per stuffed date):

- Calories: ~120
- Protein: 2g
- Fat: 6g
- Carbohydrates: 15g
- Fiber: 2g
- Sugar: 12g (natural)
- Magnesium: 10% DV
- Potassium: 8% DV
- Iron: 6% DV

Spiced Fig Compote with Greek Yogurt

 Prep Time: 5 minutes

 Cooking Time: 10-12 minutes

 Servings: 2

This warm Mediterranean-inspired dessert combines stewed dried figs with cinnamon and cloves, served over creamy Greek yogurt. Naturally sweet and rich in fiber, calcium, and antioxidants, it's perfect for digestion, heart health, and a cozy, low-sugar treat.

Ingredients:

- 6 dried figs, chopped
- 1/2 cup water
- 1/2 tsp ground cinnamon
- 1/8 tsp ground cloves
- 1/2 tsp orange zest (optional)
- 1 cup plain Greek yogurt (full-fat or low-fat)
- Optional: chopped walnuts or pistachios for topping

Instructions:

1. In a small saucepan, combine chopped figs, water, cinnamon, cloves, and optional orange zest.
2. Bring to a simmer over medium heat.
3. Reduce heat and cook for 10-12 minutes, stirring occasionally, until the figs are soft and the mixture thickens into a compote.
4. Divide the Greek yogurt between two bowls.
5. Spoon the warm fig compote over the top and add nuts if desired.
6. Serve immediately or chill and enjoy cold.

Nutrition Breakdown (per serving):

- Calories: ~220
- Protein: 10g
- Fat: 7g
- Carbohydrates: 28g
- Fiber: 4g
- Sugar: 19g (natural)
- Calcium: 15% DV
- Potassium: 10% DV
- Antioxidants: High

CHAPTER 6: DESSERTS

Sesame-Honey Bars (Pasteli)

Prep Time: 5 minutes

Cooking Time: 10 minutes

Chill Time: 30-40 minutes

Servings: 8 small bars

A naturally sweet, nutrient-dense Mediterranean snack or dessert, *Pasteli* combines toasted sesame seeds with pure honey to create a crunchy bar rich in calcium, iron, and heart-healthy fats. It's a wholesome alternative to processed sweets and ideal for seniors needing simple, nourishing energy.

Ingredients:

- 1/2 cup raw sesame seeds
- 1/4 cup raw honey
- Pinch of sea salt (optional)
- Optional: 1 tsp orange zest or 1/4 tsp ground cinnamon

Instructions:

1. Toast sesame seeds in a dry skillet over medium heat for 2-3 minutes, stirring constantly, until golden and fragrant. Remove from heat.
2. In a small saucepan, gently heat honey over low heat until it begins to bubble slightly (about 2 minutes).
3. Stir in toasted sesame seeds, salt, and any optional flavorings.
4. Pour the mixture onto parchment paper and press into a thin, even rectangle using a spatula or another sheet of parchment on top.
5. Let cool at room temperature or refrigerate for 30-40 minutes until set.
6. Cut into small bars or squares and store in an airtight container at room temp for up to 1 week.

Nutrition Breakdown (per bar):

- Calories: ~110
- Protein: 2g
- Fat: 6g
- Carbohydrates: 11g
- Fiber: 1g
- Sugar: 8g (natural)
- Calcium: 10% DV
- Iron: 8% DV
- Magnesium: 6% DV

Apricot & Almond Couscous Pudding

 Prep Time: 5 minutes

 Cooking Time: 5 minutes

 Chill Time (Optional): 15-30 minutes

 Servings: 2

This quick, gently sweetened pudding is made with fluffy couscous, tender dried apricots, and toasted almonds. Lightly infused with orange and cinnamon, it's a Mediterranean twist on traditional pudding that supports digestion, steady energy, and gentle sweetness without refined sugar.

Ingredients:

- 1/2 cup whole wheat couscous
- 1/2 cup unsweetened almond milk (or water)
- 1/4 cup chopped dried apricots
- 1 tbsp sliced or slivered almonds
- 1/2 tsp ground cinnamon
- Zest of 1/2 orange
- 1/2 tsp vanilla extract
- Optional: 1 tsp honey or maple syrup

Instructions:

1. In a small saucepan, bring almond milk to a light simmer.
2. Remove from heat and stir in couscous, apricots, cinnamon, orange zest, vanilla, and optional sweetener.
3. Cover and let sit for 5 minutes.
4. Fluff with a fork and stir in almonds.
5. Serve warm, or chill in the fridge for 15-30 minutes for a cool pudding-like texture.

Nutrition Breakdown (per serving):

- Calories: ~210
- Protein: 5g
- Fat: 6g
- Carbohydrates: 35g
- Fiber: 4g
- Sugar: 11g (mostly natural)
- Iron: 10% DV
- Vitamin A: 25% DV
- Magnesium: 10% DV

CHAPTER 7: EVERYDAY SNACKS

Hummus with Veggie Sticks

 Prep Time: 10 minutes

 Cooking Time: 0 minutes

 Servings: 4 (as a snack or appetizer)

Creamy, protein-packed hummus pairs perfectly with fresh, crunchy vegetables for a heart-healthy Mediterranean snack. It's high in fiber, plant-based protein, and good fats—making it ideal for steady energy, digestion, and brain health in older adults.

Ingredients:

For the Hummus:
- 1 can (15 oz) chickpeas, drained and rinsed
- 2 tbsp tahini
- 2 tbsp extra virgin olive oil
- Juice of 1 lemon
- 1 small clove garlic, minced
- 2–3 tbsp cold water (as needed for consistency)
- 1/2 tsp ground cumin (optional)
- Salt to taste

For the Veggie Sticks:
- 1 carrot, peeled and cut into sticks
- 1 cucumber, sliced into rounds or sticks
- 1 bell pepper, sliced
- 1 celery stalk, cut into sticks
- Optional: radishes, cherry tomatoes, snap peas

Instructions:

1. Make the hummus: In a food processor, blend chickpeas, tahini, olive oil, lemon juice, garlic, cumin (if using), and a pinch of salt until smooth.
2. Add cold water one tablespoon at a time until creamy and well blended. Taste and adjust seasoning.
3. Prep the veggies: Wash, peel, and slice vegetables into dippable shapes.
4. Serve hummus in a small bowl surrounded by veggie sticks. Drizzle with olive oil and sprinkle with paprika or parsley if desired.

Nutrition Breakdown (per serving):

- Calories: ~180
- Protein: 5g
- Fat: 11g
- Carbohydrates: 15g
- Fiber: 4g
- Sugar: 3g
- Sodium: 180mg
- Folate: 15% DV
- Vitamin A & C: High
- Gluten-Free: Yes

CHAPTER 7: EVERYDAY SNACKS

Stuffed Grape Leaves (Dolmas)

Prep Time: 25 minutes
Cooking Time: 35 minutes
Servings: 20 small dolmas (about 4 servings)

A traditional Mediterranean appetizer, dolmas are tender grape leaves filled with a fragrant mixture of rice, herbs, and lemon. They're light, flavorful, and rich in fiber and antioxidants—perfect for healthy aging and digestion support.

Ingredients:

- 1 jar (about 8 oz) grape leaves in brine (about 25-30 leaves)
- 1 cup cooked white or brown rice
- 2 tbsp olive oil (plus more for drizzling)
- Juice of 1 lemon
- 2 tbsp chopped fresh parsley
- 1 tbsp chopped fresh dill or mint
- 1 small onion, finely chopped
- Salt and pepper to taste
- Optional: pine nuts or currants (1 tbsp each)

Instructions:

1. Prepare the grape leaves: Rinse under cold water to remove excess brine. Pat dry. Set aside.
2. In a skillet, heat 1 tbsp olive oil and sauté onion until soft (about 4-5 minutes). Remove from heat.
3. In a bowl, combine cooked rice, sautéed onion, herbs, lemon juice, remaining olive oil, salt, and pepper. Add pine nuts or currants if using.
4. Lay one grape leaf flat, shiny side down. Place about 1 tablespoon of filling near the stem end.
5. Fold the sides over and roll tightly into a small cylinder. Repeat with remaining leaves and filling.
6. Arrange stuffed leaves seam-side down in a single layer in a saucepan.
7. Add enough water to just cover the dolmas, drizzle with olive oil, and weigh them down with a heatproof plate.
8. Simmer over low heat for 30-35 minutes until tender. Cool to room temperature.
9. Serve chilled or at room temperature with lemon wedges.

Nutrition Breakdown (per serving – about 5 dolmas):

- Calories: ~180
- Protein: 3g
- Fat: 8g
- Carbohydrates: 24g
- Fiber: 3g
- Sugar: 1g
- Sodium: 220mg
- Vitamin K: 60% DV
- Iron: 10% DV
- Antioxidants: High

Cucumber & Feta Bites

 Prep Time: 10 minutes

 Cooking Time: 0 minutes

 Servings: 4 (makes 12-16 bites)

These fresh and savory bites pair crisp cucumber rounds with creamy feta and a touch of Mediterranean herbs. Light and low in carbs, they're a refreshing snack or appetizer that supports hydration, bone health, and heart wellness—ideal for seniors seeking easy-to-eat, nutritious foods.

Ingredients:

- 1 large cucumber, sliced into 1/2-inch rounds
- 1/3 cup crumbled feta cheese
- 1 tbsp plain Greek yogurt (to help bind, optional)
- 1 tsp extra virgin olive oil
- 1/2 tsp dried oregano or chopped fresh dill
- Fresh ground black pepper to taste
- Optional: cherry tomato halves, fresh mint leaves, or pitted kalamata olive slices for topping

Instructions:

1. In a small bowl, mix feta, yogurt (if using), olive oil, and oregano or dill until it forms a spreadable mixture.
2. Place cucumber rounds on a platter.
3. Top each slice with about 1 teaspoon of the feta mixture.
4. Garnish with black pepper and optional toppings like tomato halves, mint, or olive slices.
5. Serve immediately or chill for up to 1 hour before serving.

Nutrition Breakdown (per 4 bites):

- Calories: ~90
- Protein: 4g
- Fat: 6g
- Carbohydrates: 3g
- Fiber: 0.5g
- Sugar: 1g
- Sodium: 180mg
- Calcium: 12% DV
- Hydration: Excellent
- Gluten-Free: Yes

CHAPTER 7: EVERYDAY SNACKS

Mini Caprese Skewers

 Prep Time: 10 minutes

 Cooking Time: 0 minutes

 Servings: 4 (makes 12 skewers)

These colorful Mediterranean-inspired skewers are a simple and elegant combination of cherry tomatoes, mozzarella, and basil. They're rich in antioxidants, calcium, and healthy fats—making them a refreshing, heart-healthy appetizer or snack that's quick to prepare and easy to eat.

Ingredients:

- 12 cherry or grape tomatoes
- 12 mini mozzarella balls (bocconcini or ciliegine)
- 12 small fresh basil leaves
- 1 tbsp extra virgin olive oil
- 1 tsp balsamic vinegar or glaze (optional)
- Salt and pepper to taste
- 12 toothpicks or small skewers

Instructions:

1. Assemble each skewer by layering one tomato, one basil leaf, and one mozzarella ball.
2. Arrange on a serving platter.
3. Drizzle olive oil and optional balsamic over the top.
4. Sprinkle lightly with salt and freshly ground black pepper.
5. Serve immediately or refrigerate for up to 2 hours before serving.

Nutrition Breakdown (per 3 skewers):

- **Calories:** ~120
- **Protein:** 6g
- **Fat:** 9g
- **Carbohydrates:** 3g
- **Fiber:** 1g
- **Sugar:** 2g
- **Calcium:** 10% DV
- **Vitamin C:** 15% DV
- **Antioxidants:** High

Marinated Olives with Orange Zest

 Prep Time: 5 minutes

 Marinating Time: 30 minutes or more

 Servings: 4

A flavorful and aromatic Mediterranean appetizer, this simple olive mix is infused with citrus zest, garlic, and herbs. It's rich in healthy fats, antioxidants, and anti-inflammatory compounds—perfect for heart health, brain support, and satisfying savory cravings.

Ingredients:

- 1 cup mixed olives (green, Kalamata, or your choice)
- 1 tbsp extra virgin olive oil
- Zest of 1 small orange
- 1 garlic clove, thinly sliced
- 1/2 tsp dried oregano or thyme
- 1/2 tsp red pepper flakes (optional)
- Optional: 1 sprig fresh rosemary or a few crushed fennel seeds

Instructions:

1. In a small bowl, combine olives, olive oil, orange zest, garlic, herbs, and any optional flavorings.
2. Toss well to coat and let marinate at room temperature for at least 30 minutes to allow flavors to meld.
3. Serve in a small dish. Leftovers can be refrigerated for up to 5 days (bring to room temperature before serving for best flavor).

Nutrition Breakdown (per serving):

- Calories: ~100
- Protein: 0g
- Fat: 10g
- Carbohydrates: 2g
- Fiber: 1g
- Sugar: 0g
- Sodium: ~350mg
- Antioxidants: High
- Vitamin E: 8% DV

CHAPTER 7: EVERYDAY SNACKS

Roasted Red Pepper Hummus

 Prep Time: 10 minutes

 Cooking Time: 0 minutes (if using jarred peppers)

 Servings: 4

This vibrant twist on classic hummus adds sweetness and smokiness from roasted red peppers. Rich in fiber, plant-based protein, and antioxidants like vitamin C and beta-carotene, it's a flavorful and heart-healthy Mediterranean dip perfect for veggies, pita, or crackers.

Ingredients:

- 1 can (15 oz) chickpeas, drained and rinsed
- 1 large roasted red pepper (jarred or homemade)
- 2 tbsp tahini
- 2 tbsp extra virgin olive oil
- Juice of 1 lemon
- 1 garlic clove
- 1/2 tsp ground cumin (optional)
- Salt to taste
- 2-3 tbsp cold water (as needed for consistency)

Instructions:

1. Add chickpeas, roasted red pepper, tahini, lemon juice, garlic, cumin (if using), and a pinch of salt to a food processor.
2. Blend until smooth, scraping down the sides as needed.
3. With the motor running, drizzle in olive oil and add water gradually until desired texture is reached.
4. Taste and adjust seasoning.
5. Serve with a drizzle of olive oil, a sprinkle of paprika, and fresh veggies or whole grain pita.

Nutrition Breakdown (per serving):

- Calories: ~180
- Protein: 5g
- Fat: 10g
- Carbohydrates: 16g
- Fiber: 4g
- Sugar: 2g
- Sodium: 180mg
- Vitamin C: 25% DV
- Folate: 20% DV
- Gluten-Free: Yes

Whole Grain Pita with Tzatziki

 Prep Time: 10 minutes

 Cooking Time: 0 minutes (unless toasting pita)

 Servings: 4

This refreshing and creamy yogurt-cucumber dip is paired with warm whole grain pita for a satisfying, fiber-rich Mediterranean snack or appetizer. Tzatziki is light, probiotic-rich, and cooling—great for digestion, hydration, and healthy aging.

Ingredients:

For the Tzatziki:
- 1 cup plain Greek yogurt (full-fat or 2%)
- 1/2 cucumber, peeled, grated, and squeezed to remove excess water
- 1 tbsp extra virgin olive oil
- 1 tbsp fresh lemon juice
- 1 clove garlic, finely minced
- 1 tbsp chopped fresh dill or mint
- Salt and pepper to taste

For Serving:
- 2 whole grain pita breads, cut into wedges
- Optional: drizzle of olive oil or sprinkle of za'atar

Instructions:

1. In a mixing bowl, combine Greek yogurt, grated cucumber, olive oil, lemon juice, garlic, and herbs.
2. Stir well and season with salt and pepper to taste. Chill for 10 minutes to allow flavors to blend.
3. Meanwhile, warm or lightly toast pita wedges if desired.
4. Serve tzatziki in a bowl alongside the pita. Drizzle with a little olive oil and top with extra dill or mint if desired.

Nutrition Breakdown (per serving):

- Calories: ~200
- Protein: 8g
- Fat: 9g
- Carbohydrates: 22g
- Fiber: 3g
- Sugar: 3g
- Calcium: 10% DV
- Probiotics: Present
- Hydration: Excellent

CHAPTER 7: EVERYDAY SNACKS

Spiced Roasted Chickpeas

 Prep Time: 5 minutes

 Cooking Time: 30-35 minutes

 Servings: 4

Crunchy, savory, and protein-rich, these roasted chickpeas make a satisfying Mediterranean snack or appetizer. Seasoned with olive oil and warming spices, they support blood sugar balance, heart health, and long-lasting energy—perfect for a grab-and-go bite.

Ingredients:

- 1 can (15 oz) chickpeas, drained, rinsed, and patted very dry
- 1 tbsp olive oil
- 1/2 tsp ground cumin
- 1/2 tsp smoked paprika
- 1/4 tsp garlic powder
- 1/4 tsp sea salt
- Optional: pinch of cayenne or turmeric

Instructions:

1. Preheat oven to 400°F (200°C). Line a baking sheet with parchment paper.
2. Spread chickpeas out on a clean kitchen towel or paper towel and pat them very dry—this helps with crispiness.
3. Toss chickpeas in olive oil and seasonings until well coated.
4. Spread them in a single layer on the baking sheet.
5. Roast for 30-35 minutes, shaking the pan once or twice, until golden and crispy.
6. Let cool for 5 minutes—they'll continue to crisp as they cool.
7. Enjoy warm or at room temperature. Store in an airtight container for up to 3 days.

Nutrition Breakdown (per serving):

- Calories: ~160
- Protein: 6g
- Fat: 7g
- Carbohydrates: 18g
- Fiber: 5g
- Sugar: 1g
- Sodium: 160mg
- Folate: 25% DV
- Iron: 10% DV
- Gluten-Free: Yes

Greek Yogurt & Herb Dip with Crackers

 Prep Time: 5 minutes

 Cooking Time: 0 minutes

 Servings: 4

This creamy, protein-rich dip is made with Greek yogurt, lemon, garlic, and fresh herbs. Light and refreshing, it pairs perfectly with whole grain or seed crackers for a Mediterranean snack that supports gut health, bone strength, and steady energy.

Ingredients:

- 1 cup plain Greek yogurt (full-fat or 2%)
- 1 tbsp extra virgin olive oil
- 1 tbsp fresh lemon juice
- 1 small garlic clove, minced
- 1 tbsp chopped fresh dill (or parsley, mint, or chives)
- Salt and pepper to taste
- Optional: pinch of crushed red pepper or lemon zest
- Whole grain or seed crackers for serving

Instructions:

1. In a bowl, whisk together the Greek yogurt, olive oil, lemon juice, and garlic.
2. Stir in fresh herbs and season with salt and pepper.
3. Let sit for 5-10 minutes to allow the flavors to develop.
4. Serve in a small dish alongside crackers or crisp veggies.
5. Optional: drizzle with a little olive oil and garnish with more herbs or lemon zest.

Nutrition Breakdown (per serving, not including crackers):

- Calories: ~120
- Protein: 9g
- Fat: 7g
- Carbohydrates: 4g
- Fiber: 0g
- Sugar: 2g
- Calcium: 12% DV
- Probiotics: Present
- Gluten-Free: Yes (if using GF crackers)

CHAPTER 7: EVERYDAY SNACKS

Baba Ghanoush with Seed Crackers

Prep Time: 10 minutes

Cooking Time: 30-35 minutes (for roasting eggplant)

Servings: 4

Baba Ghanoush is a smoky, creamy eggplant dip that's naturally low in carbs and high in fiber and antioxidants. Paired with crunchy seed crackers, it makes for a gut-friendly, heart-healthy Mediterranean appetizer that's both satisfying and nutrient-dense.

Ingredients:

For the Baba Ghanoush:
- 1 large eggplant
- 2 tbsp tahini
- 1 tbsp extra virgin olive oil
- Juice of 1 lemon
- 1 garlic clove
- 1/4 tsp ground cumin (optional)
- Salt to taste
- Optional garnish: olive oil drizzle, smoked paprika, chopped parsley

For Serving:
- Seed crackers (store-bought or homemade)

Instructions:

1. Roast the eggplant: Preheat oven to 400°F (200°C). Prick eggplant with a fork and roast on a baking sheet for 30-35 minutes until collapsed and tender. Let cool slightly.
2. Scoop out the soft flesh and place in a food processor or bowl.
3. Add tahini, olive oil, lemon juice, garlic, cumin, and salt.
4. Blend or mash until smooth but slightly rustic in texture. Taste and adjust seasoning.
5. Serve in a bowl, drizzled with olive oil and garnished as desired.
6. Enjoy with seed crackers or raw veggies.

Nutrition Breakdown (per serving, not including crackers):

- Calories: ~130
- Protein: 3g
- Fat: 10g
- Carbohydrates: 9g
- Fiber: 4g
- Sugar: 3g
- Vitamin C: 10% DV
- Potassium: 10% DV
- Antioxidants: High
- Gluten-Free: Yes

Mini Falafel Balls with Tahini Sauce

Prep Time: 15 minutes

Cooking Time: 25 minutes (baked version)

Servings: 4 (makes about 12 mini falafel)

These bite-sized baked falafel are packed with herbs, garlic, and chickpeas for a crispy-on-the-outside, tender-on-the-inside snack. Paired with a creamy lemon-tahini sauce, they're high in fiber, plant-based protein, and anti-inflammatory ingredients—perfect for heart health and sustained energy.

Ingredients:

For the Falafel:
- 1 can (15 oz) chickpeas, drained and rinsed
- 1/4 cup fresh parsley or cilantro
- 1 garlic clove
- 1/4 cup onion, chopped
- 2 tbsp oat flour or breadcrumbs
- 1/2 tsp ground cumin
- 1/4 tsp ground coriander
- Salt and pepper to taste
- 1 tbsp olive oil (for brushing or drizzling)

For the Tahini Sauce:
- 2 tbsp tahini
- 1 tbsp fresh lemon juice
- 1 tbsp water (plus more to thin)
- Pinch of garlic powder or minced garlic
- Salt to taste

Instructions:

1. Preheat oven to 375°F (190°C). Line a baking sheet with parchment.
2. In a food processor, combine chickpeas, herbs, garlic, onion, spices, and flour. Pulse until well combined but still slightly chunky.
3. Roll into 1-inch balls and place on the baking sheet. Brush or drizzle with olive oil.
4. Bake for 25 minutes, flipping halfway, until golden and firm.
5. Meanwhile, whisk together tahini sauce ingredients until smooth and creamy. Thin with more water if needed.
6. Serve falafel warm with tahini sauce for dipping.

Nutrition Breakdown (per 3 mini falafel + sauce):

- Calories: ~170
- Protein: 6g
- Fat: 9g
- Carbohydrates: 15g
- Fiber: 4g
- Sugar: 1g
- Iron: 10% DV
- Folate: 20% DV
- Gluten-Free: Yes (if using GF flour)

CHAPTER 7: EVERYDAY SNACKS

Tomato Bruschetta on Whole Grain Toast

 Prep Time: 10 minutes

 Cooking Time: 5 minutes (to toast bread)

 Servings: 4 (makes 8 pieces)

A Mediterranean favorite, this version of bruschetta uses juicy tomatoes, garlic, and basil served on hearty whole grain toast. It's rich in antioxidants, fiber, and healthy fats—perfect as a refreshing appetizer or snack to support heart and brain health.

Ingredients:

- 4 slices whole grain bread, halved (to make 8 pieces)
- 2 medium tomatoes, finely chopped
- 1 small garlic clove, minced
- 1 tbsp extra virgin olive oil (plus more for brushing)
- 1 tbsp fresh basil, chopped
- Salt and black pepper to taste
- Optional: balsamic glaze or a sprinkle of Parmesan

Instructions:

1. Toast or grill the bread slices until golden and crisp.
2. In a bowl, mix chopped tomatoes, garlic, olive oil, basil, salt, and pepper. Let sit for 5-10 minutes to marinate.
3. Lightly brush toasted bread with olive oil.
4. Spoon the tomato mixture onto each piece of toast.
5. Drizzle with balsamic glaze or sprinkle with Parmesan if desired.
6. Serve immediately while the bread is still crisp.

Nutrition Breakdown (per 2 pieces):

- Calories: ~160
- Protein: 4g
- Fat: 8g
- Carbohydrates: 18g
- Fiber: 4g
- Sugar: 3g
- Vitamin C: 20% DV
- Lycopene: High
- Whole Grains: Yes

Zucchini Fritters with Yogurt Dip

Prep Time: 15 minutes

Cooking Time: 10-12 minutes

Servings: 4 (makes about 8 fritters)

These light and crispy zucchini fritters are packed with veggies and Mediterranean herbs, lightly pan-fried for a golden finish. Served with a creamy yogurt dip, they make a fiber-rich, anti-inflammatory snack or appetizer that's easy to digest and full of flavor.

Ingredients:

For the Fritters:
- 2 medium zucchinis, grated
- 1/4 tsp salt
- 1 egg
- 1/4 cup crumbled feta cheese
- 1/4 cup whole wheat flour (or chickpea flour)
- 1 tbsp chopped parsley or dill
- 1 clove garlic, minced
- 2 tbsp olive oil (for pan-frying)
- Black pepper to taste

For the Yogurt Dip:
- 1/2 cup plain Greek yogurt
- 1 tbsp lemon juice
- 1 tsp chopped dill or mint
- Salt and pepper to taste

Instructions:

1. Grate the zucchini and sprinkle with salt. Let sit for 5-10 minutes, then squeeze out excess moisture using a clean towel.
2. In a bowl, mix zucchini, egg, feta, flour, herbs, garlic, and pepper until combined.
3. Heat olive oil in a skillet over medium heat. Scoop 2-tbsp portions of the batter and flatten into small patties.
4. Cook for 3-4 minutes per side until golden brown and crisp. Remove and drain on paper towels.
5. Mix all dip ingredients in a bowl until smooth.
6. Serve fritters warm with yogurt dip on the side.

Nutrition Breakdown (per 2 fritters + dip):

- Calories: ~180
- Protein: 7g
- Fat: 10g
- Carbohydrates: 14g
- Fiber: 2g
- Sugar: 3g
- Calcium: 12% DV
- Vitamin A & C: High
- Gluten-Free: Optional

CHAPTER 7: EVERYDAY SNACKS

Hard-Boiled Eggs with Olive Tapenade

 Prep Time: 10 minutes

 Cooking Time: 10 minutes

 Servings: 4 (2 egg halves per person)

A protein-rich Mediterranean snack, this savory combo pairs creamy hard-boiled eggs with bold, briny olive tapenade. It's full of healthy fats, choline, and antioxidants—perfect for supporting brain health, energy, and satiety in a simple, elegant bite.

Ingredients:

For the Eggs:
- 4 large eggs
- Salt and pepper to taste

For the Tapenade:
- 1/3 cup pitted Kalamata olives
- 1 tsp capers
- 1 tsp lemon juice
- 1 tsp olive oil
- 1 small garlic clove (optional)
- Black pepper to taste

Instructions:

1. Boil the eggs: Place eggs in a saucepan and cover with cold water. Bring to a boil, then reduce heat and simmer for 10 minutes. Transfer to an ice bath to cool. Peel and halve.
2. Make the tapenade: Add olives, capers, lemon juice, olive oil, and optional garlic to a food processor or finely chop by hand. Pulse until chunky-smooth. Season with pepper.
3. Spoon a small dollop of tapenade onto each egg half.
4. Serve chilled or at room temperature.

Nutrition Breakdown (per serving – 2 halves):

- Calories: ~120
- Protein: 6g
- Fat: 9g
- Carbohydrates: 1g
- Fiber: 0.5g
- Sugar: 0g
- Sodium: ~210mg
- Choline: 35% DV
- Omega-3s: Present
- Gluten-Free: Yes

Lentil & Herb Salad Cups

Prep Time: 10 minutes

Cooking Time: 20 minutes (if cooking lentils from dry)

Servings: 4 (makes 8 lettuce cups)

These crisp and refreshing salad cups are filled with a tangy lentil mixture rich in protein, fiber, and anti-inflammatory herbs. Served in crunchy lettuce leaves, they make a light and energizing Mediterranean appetizer—great for digestion and steady blood sugar support.

Ingredients:

- 1 cup cooked green or brown lentils (or 1/2 cup dry, cooked and cooled)
- 2 tbsp extra virgin olive oil
- 1 tbsp lemon juice
- 1 tbsp chopped fresh parsley
- 1 tbsp chopped fresh mint or dill
- 1 small tomato, finely chopped
- 1/4 small red onion, finely chopped
- Salt and black pepper to taste
- 8 small romaine or butter lettuce leaves (for cups)
- Optional: crumbled feta or chopped walnuts for topping

Instructions:

1. In a mixing bowl, combine cooked lentils, olive oil, lemon juice, herbs, tomato, and red onion.
2. Toss gently to combine. Season with salt and pepper to taste.
3. Spoon 2-3 tablespoons of the mixture into each lettuce leaf.
4. Top with crumbled feta or walnuts if desired.
5. Serve chilled or at room temperature as a handheld snack or plated appetizer.

Nutrition Breakdown (per 2 salad cups):

- Calories: ~140
- Protein: 6g
- Fat: 6g
- Carbohydrates: 15g
- Fiber: 5g
- Sugar: 2g
- Iron: 15% DV
- Folate: 35% DV
- Vitamin A: 40% DV

CHAPTER 7: EVERYDAY SNACKS

Ricotta-Stuffed Cherry Tomatoes

 Prep Time: 10 minutes

 Cooking Time: 0 minutes

 Servings: 4 (makes about 12 stuffed tomatoes)

These bite-sized Mediterranean appetizers are bursting with flavor and nutrients. Juicy cherry tomatoes are filled with creamy ricotta and fresh herbs for a light, low-carb snack that's rich in calcium and supports digestion, bone strength, and immune health.

Ingredients:

- 12 cherry tomatoes
- 1/2 cup ricotta cheese (whole milk or part-skim)
- 1 tbsp fresh basil or parsley, finely chopped
- 1/2 tsp lemon zest
- Salt and black pepper to taste
- Optional: drizzle of olive oil or balsamic glaze

Instructions:

1. Slice the tops off the cherry tomatoes and carefully scoop out the insides using a small spoon or knife.
2. In a small bowl, mix ricotta, chopped herbs, lemon zest, salt, and pepper until smooth.
3. Spoon or pipe the ricotta mixture into each hollowed tomato.
4. Arrange on a platter and drizzle lightly with olive oil or balsamic if desired.
5. Chill for 10-15 minutes before serving, or serve immediately.

Nutrition Breakdown (per 3 stuffed tomatoes):

- Calories: ~90
- Protein: 4g
- Fat: 6g
- Carbohydrates: 4g
- Fiber: 1g
- Sugar: 2g
- Calcium: 10% DV
- Vitamin C: 15% DV
- Gluten-Free: Yes

Mini Spinach & Feta Phyllo Triangles

 Prep Time: 20 minutes

 Cooking Time: 20-25 minutes

 Servings: 6 (makes about 12 triangles)

Inspired by the Greek classic spanakopita, these crisp and flaky phyllo triangles are filled with a savory blend of spinach, feta, and herbs. They're rich in calcium, iron, and flavor—perfect for a warm Mediterranean appetizer or snack that feels indulgent but nourishes deeply.

Ingredients:

- 1/2 package phyllo dough, thawed
- 1 1/2 cups fresh spinach (or 3/4 cup thawed frozen spinach), chopped
- 1/2 cup crumbled feta cheese
- 1 egg
- 1 green onion, finely chopped
- 1 tbsp chopped fresh dill or parsley
- Salt and pepper to taste
- 2 tbsp olive oil (or melted butter) for brushing

Instructions:

1. Preheat oven to 375°F (190°C). Line a baking sheet with parchment paper.
2. Prepare filling: In a bowl, mix spinach, feta, egg, green onion, herbs, salt, and pepper.
3. Work with phyllo dough: Keep unused sheets covered with a damp towel to prevent drying. Cut sheets into 3" wide strips.
4. Assemble triangles: Place a small spoonful of filling at one end of each strip. Fold corner over to make a triangle and continue folding, like a flag, until sealed. Brush lightly with olive oil.
5. Bake for 20-25 minutes, or until golden and crisp.
6. Cool slightly before serving. Serve warm or at room temperature.

Nutrition Breakdown (per 2 triangles):

- Calories: ~160
- Protein: 5g
- Fat: 9g
- Carbohydrates: 14g
- Fiber: 1g
- Sugar: 1g
- Calcium: 10% DV
- Iron: 8% DV
- Vitamin A: 25% DV

Smoked Salmon on Cucumber Rounds

 Prep Time: 10 minutes

 Cooking Time: 0 minutes

 Servings: 4 (makes 12 bites)

These elegant, no-cook appetizers feature crisp cucumber slices topped with creamy yogurt or cheese, delicate smoked salmon, and a touch of fresh dill. They're rich in omega-3s, protein, and antioxidants—great for heart and brain health, and easy for seniors to enjoy.

Ingredients:

- 1 large cucumber, sliced into 12 thick rounds
- 3 oz smoked salmon, sliced into 12 small pieces
- 3 tbsp Greek yogurt, cream cheese, or labneh
- 1 tsp lemon juice
- 1 tsp chopped fresh dill or chives
- Fresh ground black pepper to taste
- Optional: capers or thin lemon zest strips for garnish

Instructions:

1. Lay cucumber slices on a serving platter.
2. In a small bowl, mix yogurt (or cheese) with lemon juice and herbs.
3. Spoon or pipe a small dollop onto each cucumber round.
4. Top each with a piece of smoked salmon.
5. Garnish with extra herbs, a crack of black pepper, and optional capers or lemon zest.
6. Serve immediately or refrigerate until ready to serve (up to 1 hour for best texture).

Nutrition Breakdown (per 3 bites):

- Calories: ~110
- Protein: **7g**
- Fat: **6g**
- Carbohydrates: **4g**
- Fiber: **1g**
- Sugar: **1g**
- Omega-3s: **High**
- Sodium: **~180mg**
- Vitamin D: **20% DV**

Warm Herbed Olives & Almonds

 Prep Time: 5 minutes

 Cooking Time: 5-7 minutes

 Servings: 4

This savory Mediterranean snack blends briny olives and toasty almonds with warming herbs and citrus zest. Served warm, it's perfect for entertaining or as a satisfying, heart-healthy nibble rich in good fats, fiber, and antioxidants.

Ingredients:

- 1/2 cup mixed olives (green, black, or Kalamata)
- 1/3 cup raw almonds
- 1 tbsp extra virgin olive oil
- 1 strip of lemon or orange zest (use a vegetable peeler)
- 1 sprig fresh rosemary or 1/2 tsp dried
- 1 garlic clove, thinly sliced
- Pinch of red pepper flakes (optional)

Instructions:

1. In a skillet, heat olive oil over medium heat.
2. Add almonds and cook for 1-2 minutes, stirring, until they start to lightly toast.
3. Add garlic, rosemary, lemon/orange zest, and olives.
4. Sauté for another 3-4 minutes, stirring occasionally, until everything is fragrant and warmed through.
5. Add a pinch of red pepper flakes if desired, and remove from heat.
6. Serve warm in a small bowl with toothpicks or spooned over crostini.

Nutrition Breakdown (per serving):

- Calories: ~160
- Protein: 3g
- Fat: 15g
- Carbohydrates: 4g
- Fiber: 2g
- Sugar: 0g
- Vitamin E: 15% DV
- Antioxidants: High
- Sodium: ~200mg

CHAPTER 7: EVERYDAY SNACKS

Mini Bell Peppers Stuffed with Hummus

Prep Time: 10 minutes

Cooking Time: 0 minutes

Servings: 4 (makes about 12 halves)

These colorful, crunchy peppers are stuffed with creamy hummus for a vibrant, low-carb Mediterranean snack. Rich in fiber, protein, and antioxidants, they're perfect for boosting energy and supporting heart and digestive health in a fun, easy-to-eat format.

Ingredients:

- 6 mini bell peppers, halved and seeded
- 1/2 cup plain hummus (store-bought or homemade)
- Optional toppings: paprika, chopped parsley, sesame seeds, or pine nuts

Instructions:

1. Slice mini bell peppers in half lengthwise and remove seeds.
2. Spoon about 2 teaspoons of hummus into each pepper half.
3. Sprinkle with optional toppings for extra flavor and presentation.
4. Serve immediately or refrigerate for up to 2 hours before serving.

Nutrition Breakdown (per 3 halves):

- Calories: ~100
- Protein: 4g
- Fat: 5g
- Carbohydrates: 10g
- Fiber: 3g
- Sugar: 4g
- Vitamin C: 100% DV
- Folate: 10% DV
- Gluten-Free: Yes

CHAPTER 8: SMOOTHIES, TEAS & JUICES

CHAPTER 8: SMOOTHIES, TEAS & JUICES

Spinach, Banana & Olive Oil Smoothie

 Prep Time: 5 minutes

 Cooking Time: 0 minutes

 Servings: 1

This vibrant green smoothie blends leafy greens, creamy banana, and a splash of extra virgin olive oil for a drink that supports energy, digestion, and inflammation reduction. It's perfect for a light breakfast or mid-day reset, especially for seniors looking to support heart and brain health.

Ingredients:

- 1 cup fresh spinach
- 1 small ripe banana
- 3/4 cup unsweetened almond milk (or water)
- 1 tbsp extra virgin olive oil
- 1/2 tsp ground flaxseed or chia seeds (optional)
- 1/4 tsp cinnamon (optional)
- 2-3 ice cubes (optional for texture)

Instructions:

1. Add all ingredients to a blender.
2. Blend until completely smooth, about 30-45 seconds.
3. Taste and adjust with more cinnamon or a splash of lemon juice if desired.
4. Serve immediately and enjoy fresh.

Nutrition Breakdown (per serving):

- Calories: ~230
- Protein: 3g
- Fat: 14g
- Carbohydrates: 22g
- Fiber: 5g
- Sugar: 10g (natural)
- Vitamin K: 150% DV
- Potassium: 15% DV
- Omega-3s: Present

Fig & Almond Smoothie

 Prep Time: 5 minutes

 Cooking Time: 0 minutes

 Servings: 1

This smooth and satisfying blend features sweet dried figs, creamy almond milk, and warming cinnamon. Rich in fiber, calcium, and antioxidants, it supports digestion, bone health, and blood sugar balance—making it a perfect energizing snack or light breakfast.

Ingredients:

- 3-4 dried figs, stems removed
- 3/4 cup unsweetened almond milk
- 1 tbsp almond butter (or a small handful of raw almonds)
- 1/2 frozen banana (optional, for added creaminess)
- 1/4 tsp cinnamon
- 1/4 tsp vanilla extract (optional)
- 2-3 ice cubes

Instructions:

1. Soak figs in warm water for 5 minutes to soften (if needed).
2. Add all ingredients to a blender.
3. Blend until smooth and creamy, about 30 seconds.
4. Pour into a glass and enjoy immediately.

Nutrition Breakdown (per serving):

- Calories: ~250
- Protein: 4g
- Fat: 10g
- Carbohydrates: 35g
- Fiber: 6g
- Sugar: 24g (natural)
- Calcium: 20% DV
- Magnesium: 15% DV
- Iron: 10% DV

CHAPTER 8: SMOOTHIES, TEAS & JUICES

Greek Yogurt & Berry Smoothie

 Prep Time: 5 minutes

 Cooking Time: 0 minutes

 Servings: 1

This antioxidant-rich smoothie combines probiotic Greek yogurt with a mix of berries for a gut-friendly, protein-packed blend that supports immunity, digestion, and healthy aging. It's perfect as a quick breakfast, post-walk snack, or afternoon refresher.

Ingredients:

- 1/2 cup plain Greek yogurt (full-fat or 2%)
- 1/2 cup frozen mixed berries (strawberries, blueberries, raspberries)
- 1/2 cup unsweetened almond milk (or water)
- 1/2 banana (optional, for added creaminess)
- 1/2 tsp honey or maple syrup (optional, if extra sweetness desired)
- 1/4 tsp vanilla extract
- Ice cubes (optional, for texture)

Instructions:

1. Add all ingredients to a blender.
2. Blend until thick and creamy.
3. Pour into a glass and enjoy immediately.

Nutrition Breakdown (per serving):

- Calories: ~180
- Protein: 10g
- Fat: 5g
- Carbohydrates: 22g
- Fiber: 4g
- Sugar: 14g (mostly natural)
- Calcium: 15% DV
- Probiotics: Present
- Antioxidants: High

Avocado-Cucumber Mint Smoothie

 Prep Time: 5 minutes

 Cooking Time: 0 minutes

 Servings: 1

This creamy green smoothie blends heart-healthy avocado with cooling cucumber and fresh mint. Packed with fiber, healthy fats, and electrolytes, it's a perfect Mediterranean-inspired drink for hydration, digestion, and skin health—especially on warm days or after light movement.

Ingredients:

- 1/2 ripe avocado
- 1/2 cucumber, peeled and chopped
- 3/4 cup cold water or unsweetened almond milk
- 4-5 fresh mint leaves
- Juice of 1/2 lemon
- Pinch of sea salt
- Ice cubes (optional, for chill and texture)

Instructions:

1. Add all ingredients to a blender.
2. Blend on high until smooth and creamy.
3. Taste and adjust with more lemon or mint as desired.
4. Serve chilled.

Nutrition Breakdown (per serving):

- Calories: ~160
- Protein: 2g
- Fat: 12g
- Carbohydrates: 12g
- Fiber: 6g
- Sugar: 2g
- Potassium: 15% DV
- Vitamin K: 40% DV
- Hydration: Excellent

CHAPTER 8: SMOOTHIES, TEAS & JUICES

Orange-Date Smoothie with Tahini

 Prep Time: 5 minutes

 Cooking Time: 0 minutes

 Servings: 1

This Mediterranean-inspired smoothie combines juicy orange, naturally sweet dates, and nutty tahini for a rich, nourishing blend. It's loaded with antioxidants, fiber, and calcium — great for steady energy, bone strength, and a comforting mid-morning or afternoon pick-me-up.

Ingredients:

- 1 large orange, peeled and segmented
- 2 Medjool dates, pitted (soaked in warm water if needed)
- 1 tbsp tahini
- 1/2 cup unsweetened almond milk or water
- 1/4 tsp cinnamon
- 1/4 tsp vanilla extract (optional)
- Ice cubes (optional, for a chilled version)

Instructions:

1. Add all ingredients to a blender.
2. Blend until completely smooth and creamy.
3. Taste and adjust with more cinnamon or a splash of lemon juice if desired.
4. Serve immediately.

Nutrition Breakdown (per serving):

- Calories: ~210
- Protein: 4g
- Fat: 8g
- Carbohydrates: 32g
- Fiber: 5g
- Sugar: 22g (natural)
- Calcium: 10% DV
- Iron: 8% DV
- Magnesium: 12% DV

Zucchini & Pineapple Smoothie

 Prep Time: 5 minutes

 Cooking Time: 0 minutes

 Servings: 1

This refreshing smoothie sneaks in hydrating zucchini and blends it with sweet pineapple for a fiber-rich, anti-inflammatory drink. It's gentle on digestion, low in sugar, and perfect for a light breakfast or cooling afternoon refresher—ideal for seniors or anyone looking for a clean, vibrant option.

Ingredients:

- 1/2 cup chopped raw zucchini (peeled if preferred)
- 1/2 cup frozen pineapple chunks
- 1/2 banana (optional, for creaminess)
- 3/4 cup water or unsweetened almond milk
- 1/2 tsp grated fresh ginger (or a pinch of ground ginger)
- 1/2 tsp lime or lemon juice (optional, for brightness)
- Ice cubes (optional)

Instructions:

1. Add all ingredients to a blender.
2. Blend until smooth and frothy.
3. Taste and adjust with more ginger or citrus as desired.
4. Serve chilled.

Nutrition Breakdown (per serving):

- Calories: ~130
- Protein: 2g
- Fat: 1g
- Carbohydrates: 30g
- Fiber: 4g
- Sugar: 16g (mostly natural)
- Vitamin C: 70% DV
- Potassium: 10% DV
- Anti-inflammatory: Yes

CHAPTER 8: SMOOTHIES, TEAS & JUICES

Cherry-Pomegranate Smoothie

 Prep Time: 5 minutes

 Cooking Time: 0 minutes

 Servings: 1

This vibrant Mediterranean-inspired smoothie combines dark cherries and pomegranate juice for a rich, anti-inflammatory drink that supports heart health, circulation, and brain function. It's perfect as a cooling snack or post-walk recovery boost.

Ingredients:

- 1/2 cup frozen dark cherries
- 1/2 cup 100% pure pomegranate juice
- 1/4 cup plain Greek yogurt (or unsweetened plant-based yogurt)
- 1/2 banana (optional, for creaminess and sweetness)
- 1/4 tsp ground cinnamon
- Ice cubes (optional)

Instructions:

1. Add all ingredients to a blender.
2. Blend until smooth and creamy.
3. Pour into a glass and enjoy immediately.

Nutrition Breakdown (per serving):

- Calories: ~170
- Protein: 4g
- Fat: 1g
- Carbohydrates: 36g
- Fiber: 4g
- Sugar: 26g (natural)
- Antioxidants: Very High
- Vitamin C: 25% DV
- Potassium: 12% DV

Watermelon-Basil Smoothie

Prep Time: 5 minutes

Cooking Time: 0 minutes

Servings: 1

This Mediterranean-style smoothie blends juicy watermelon with a touch of fresh basil and citrus for a naturally sweet, electrolyte-rich drink. It's perfect for hot days, hydration support, and healthy aging—especially for boosting circulation and reducing inflammation.

Ingredients:

- 1 1/2 cups cubed seedless watermelon (chilled or frozen)
- 4-5 fresh basil leaves
- Juice of 1/2 lime or lemon
- 1/4 cup cold water or coconut water
- Ice cubes (optional, for texture and chill)
- Optional: pinch of sea salt for extra minerals

Instructions:

1. Add all ingredients to a blender.
2. Blend until completely smooth.
3. Taste and adjust with more citrus or basil if desired.
4. Serve immediately—best enjoyed cold!

Nutrition Breakdown (per serving):

- Calories: ~60
- Protein: 1g
- Fat: 0g
- Carbohydrates: 15g
- Fiber: 1g
- Sugar: 12g (natural)
- Hydration: Excellent
- Lycopene: High
- Vitamin C: 20% DV

CHAPTER 8: SMOOTHIES, TEAS & JUICES

Pear & Ginger Smoothie

 Prep Time: 5 minutes

 Cooking Time: 0 minutes

 Servings: 1

This Mediterranean-inspired smoothie is a naturally sweet, gut-friendly option made with ripe pear and zesty ginger. It's great for calming the stomach, reducing inflammation, and delivering steady energy — perfect for a light breakfast or post-meal refresh.

Ingredients:

- 1 ripe pear, cored and chopped
- 1/2 cup unsweetened almond milk or water
- 1/4 cup plain Greek yogurt (optional for added creaminess and protein)
- 1/2 tsp grated fresh ginger (or 1/8 tsp ground ginger)
- 1/4 tsp cinnamon (optional)
- Ice cubes (optional)

Instructions:

1. Add all ingredients to a blender.
2. Blend until smooth and creamy.
3. Taste and adjust with more ginger or cinnamon if desired.
4. Serve immediately.

Nutrition Breakdown (per serving):

- Calories: ~130
- Protein: 3g
- Fat: 3g
- Carbohydrates: 25g
- Fiber: 4g
- Sugar: 15g (natural)
- Vitamin C: 12% DV
- Potassium: 10% DV
- Digestive Support: Yes

Coconut-Yogurt Smoothie with Pistachios

 Prep Time: 5 minutes

 Cooking Time: 0 minutes

 Servings: 1

This luxurious smoothie combines probiotic-rich Greek yogurt, creamy coconut milk, and heart-healthy pistachios. Naturally low in sugar and full of healthy fats, it's perfect for satiety, brain support, and a satisfying breakfast or afternoon recharge.

Ingredients:

- 1/2 cup plain Greek yogurt (or unsweetened coconut yogurt)
- 1/2 cup light coconut milk
- 1 tbsp raw pistachios (plus extra for topping)
- 1/2 banana (optional, for creaminess and subtle sweetness)
- 1/2 tsp vanilla extract
- Ice cubes (optional)

Instructions:

1. Add all ingredients to a blender.
2. Blend until smooth and creamy.
3. Pour into a glass, and sprinkle extra chopped pistachios on top if desired.
4. Serve immediately.

Nutrition Breakdown (per serving):

- Calories: ~220
- Protein: 8g
- Fat: 15g
- Carbohydrates: 14g
- Fiber: 2g
- Sugar: 7g (mostly natural)
- Calcium: 12% DV
- Magnesium: 15% DV
- Probiotics: Present

CHAPTER 8: SMOOTHIES, TEAS & JUICES

Chamomile & Lemon Balm Tea

 Prep Time: 5 minutes

 Steep Time: 5–7 minutes

 Servings: 1

This calming Mediterranean herbal tea blend helps ease stress, support sleep, and gently soothe digestion. Chamomile and lemon balm are both known for their calming, anti-inflammatory properties—making this tea a perfect evening ritual or mid-day reset.

Ingredients:

- 1 tsp dried chamomile flowers (or 1 chamomile tea bag)
- 1 tsp dried lemon balm (or 1 lemon balm tea bag)
- 1 cup hot water (just off the boil)
- Optional: slice of lemon or 1/2 tsp honey for flavor

Instructions:

1. Add chamomile and lemon balm to a tea infuser or teapot.
2. Pour hot water over the herbs and cover.
3. Steep for 5–7 minutes.
4. Strain, then add lemon or honey if desired.
5. Sip slowly and enjoy warm.

Nutrition & Benefits (per cup):

- Calories: ~5
- Caffeine-Free: Yes
- Stress Support: ✓
- Digestion: ✓
- Sleep Aid: ✓
- Antioxidants: High

Mint & Green Tea Infusion

 Prep Time: 5 minutes

 Steep Time: 3-5 minutes

 Servings: 1

This Mediterranean-style tea blends the earthy warmth of green tea with the cooling freshness of mint. It's energizing without being overstimulating and supports digestion, brain health, and metabolism—perfect for a mid-morning or early afternoon sip.

Ingredients:

- 1 green tea bag (or 1 tsp loose-leaf green tea)
- 5-6 fresh mint leaves (or 1 tsp dried mint)
- 1 cup hot water (just under boiling, about 175-185°F / 80-85°C)
- Optional: lemon slice or a drizzle of honey

Instructions:

1. Place green tea and mint leaves in a teapot or mug.
2. Pour hot water over the tea and cover.
3. Let steep for 3-5 minutes, depending on desired strength.
4. Remove tea bag or strain, and add lemon or honey if desired.
5. Serve warm or chilled over ice.

Nutrition & Benefits (per cup):

- Calories: ~5
- Caffeine: Low to Moderate
- Antioxidants: High
- Mental Clarity: ✓
- Digestive Support: ✓
- Hydration: ✓

CHAPTER 8: SMOOTHIES, TEAS & JUICES

Sage & Rosemary Herbal Tea

 Prep Time: 5 minutes

 Steep Time: 5-7 minutes

 Servings: 1

This fragrant herbal tea is a soothing blend of sage and rosemary, two Mediterranean herbs known for their memory-boosting, anti-inflammatory, and antioxidant properties. Perfect for calming the mind and enhancing circulation, this tea is ideal for a relaxing evening or mental clarity boost during the day.

Ingredients:

- 1 tsp dried sage
- 1 tsp dried rosemary
- 1 cup hot water (just off the boil)
- Optional: 1/2 tsp honey or lemon slice for flavor

Instructions:

1. Add dried sage and rosemary to a tea infuser or teapot.
2. Pour hot water over the herbs and cover.
3. Let steep for 5-7 minutes.
4. Strain, then add honey or lemon if desired.
5. Serve warm and enjoy.

Nutrition & Benefits (per cup):

- Calories: ~5
- Caffeine-Free: ✓
- Memory Support: ✓
- Circulation Boost: ✓
- Antioxidants: **High**
- Inflammation Reduction: ✓

Fennel & Licorice Root Tea

 Prep Time: 5 minutes

 Steep Time: 5-7 minutes

 Servings: 1

This naturally sweet and soothing tea blends fennel and licorice root for a calming, digestion-friendly drink. Fennel is known for reducing bloating and improving gut health, while licorice root offers a naturally sweet taste and supports immune function—making this tea a perfect post-meal or evening choice.

Ingredients:

- 1 tsp fennel seeds
- 1 tsp dried licorice root
- 1 cup hot water (just off the boil)
- Optional: slice of ginger or a drizzle of honey for extra flavor

Instructions:

1. Add fennel seeds and licorice root to a tea infuser or teapot.
2. Pour hot water over the herbs and cover.
3. Let steep for 5-7 minutes.
4. Strain, and add ginger or honey if desired.
5. Serve warm and enjoy.

Nutrition & Benefits (per cup):

- Calories: ~5
- Caffeine-Free: ✓
- Digestion Support: ✓
- Immune Boost: ✓
- Inflammation Reduction: ✓
- Hydration: ✓

CHAPTER 8: SMOOTHIES, TEAS & JUICES

Olive Leaf Tea with Lemon

 Prep Time: 5 minutes

 Steep Time: 5-7 minutes

 Servings: 1

This antioxidant-packed tea uses olive leaves, which are known for their antiviral, anti-inflammatory, and heart-supporting properties. Combined with the zesty, refreshing taste of lemon, it's a Mediterranean-inspired drink perfect for immune support, detoxing, and overall wellness.

Ingredients:

- 1 tsp dried olive leaves (or 1 olive leaf tea bag)
- 1 cup hot water
- Juice of 1/2 lemon
- Optional: 1 tsp honey for sweetness

Instructions:

1. Add olive leaves to a tea infuser or teapot.
2. Pour hot water over the leaves and cover.
3. Let steep for 5-7 minutes.
4. Strain and add lemon juice and honey if desired.
5. Serve warm or chilled.

Nutrition & Benefits (per cup):

- Calories: ~5
- Caffeine-Free: ✓
- Immune Support: ✓
- Antioxidants: High
- Heart Health: ✓
- Detoxification: ✓

Carrot, Orange & Ginger Juice

 Prep Time: 5 minutes

 Juicing Time: 5 minutes

 Servings: 1

This bright and zesty juice is a delicious blend of carrots, fresh orange, and a hint of ginger. It's packed with vitamin C, beta-carotene, and anti-inflammatory ginger—perfect for boosting your immune system and providing a natural energy boost.

Ingredients:

- 2 medium carrots, peeled
- 1 large orange, peeled
- 1-inch piece of fresh ginger, peeled
- 1/2 cup water or coconut water
- Optional: ice cubes for a chilled juice

Instructions:

1. Juice the carrots, orange, and ginger in a juicer.
2. Add water or coconut water to thin the juice as needed.
3. Stir well and serve immediately over ice, if desired.

Nutrition & Benefits (per serving):

- Calories: ~150
- Vitamin A: **250% DV**
- Vitamin C: **90% DV**
- Fiber: **4g**
- Anti-inflammatory: ✓
- Immune Support: ✓
- Hydration: ✓

CHAPTER 8: SMOOTHIES, TEAS & JUICES

Cucumber-Lemon Detox Water

 Prep Time: 5 minutes

 Infusion Time: 30 minutes (or more for stronger flavor)

 Servings: 1

This refreshing detox water combines the hydrating properties of cucumber with the cleansing benefits of lemon. It's perfect for promoting digestion, boosting hydration, and supporting detoxification—an ideal drink for any time of the day.

Ingredients:

- 1/2 cucumber, sliced thin
- 1/2 lemon, sliced thin
- 1-2 fresh mint sprigs (optional)
- 2 cups cold water
- Ice cubes (optional)

Instructions:

1. Add cucumber, lemon, and mint (if using) to a water pitcher or glass.
2. Fill with cold water and stir to combine.
3. Let infuse in the refrigerator for at least 30 minutes, or longer for a stronger flavor.
4. Serve over ice if desired.

Nutrition & Benefits (per serving):

- Calories: ~5
- Hydration: ✓
- Digestion Support: ✓
- Detoxification: ✓
- Vitamin C: **15% DV**
- Antioxidants: **Present**

Pomegranate-Mint Cooler

 Prep Time: 5 minutes

 Chill Time: 10 minutes

 Servings: 1

This refreshing drink combines the tartness of pomegranate with the coolness of mint for a hydrating, antioxidant-rich cooler. It's perfect for boosting circulation, enhancing digestion, and providing a naturally sweet, hydrating beverage.

Ingredients:

- 1/2 cup pomegranate juice (fresh or 100% pure)
- 1/2 cup cold water or sparkling water
- 5-6 fresh mint leaves
- 1 tsp honey or maple syrup (optional)
- Ice cubes (optional)

Instructions:

1. In a glass, combine pomegranate juice and cold water or sparkling water.
2. Add mint leaves and lightly crush them with a muddler or spoon to release flavor.
3. Stir in honey or maple syrup if using.
4. Add ice cubes and let chill for 10 minutes.
5. Serve immediately.

Nutrition & Benefits (per serving):

- Calories: ~70
- Antioxidants: **High**
- Hydration: ✓
- Circulation Boost: ✓
- Digestive Support: ✓
- Vitamin C: **20% DV**

CHAPTER 8: SMOOTHIES, TEAS & JUICES

Celery, Apple & Parsley Juice

 Prep Time: 5 minutes

 Juicing Time: 5 minutes

 Servings: 1

This nutrient-packed juice is made with crisp celery, sweet apple, and fresh parsley—an ideal combination for detoxification, digestion, and overall wellness. It's refreshing, alkalizing, and full of antioxidants to support a healthy immune system.

Ingredients:

- 3-4 celery stalks
- 1 apple (green apple works well for a tart taste)
- 1/2 cup fresh parsley
- 1/2 lemon, juiced
- 1/2 cup water or coconut water
- Ice cubes (optional)

Instructions:

1. Juice the celery, apple, parsley, and lemon.
2. Add water or coconut water to thin the juice as needed.
3. Stir well, taste, and adjust with more lemon if desired.
4. Serve immediately over ice, if desired.

Nutrition & Benefits (per serving):

- Calories: ~120
- Fiber: 5g
- Vitamin C: 30% DV
- Antioxidants: High
- Detoxification: ✓
- Digestion Support: ✓
- Hydration: ✓

159

Warm Lemon Water with Olive Oil

 Prep Time: 5 minutes

 Servings: 1

This simple, soothing Mediterranean drink is known for its detoxifying and digestive benefits. Warm lemon water combined with heart-healthy olive oil supports liver function, digestion, and hydration, making it a great way to start your morning.

Ingredients:

- 1 cup warm water
- Juice of 1/2 lemon
- 1 tsp extra virgin olive oil
- Optional: pinch of sea salt for added minerals

Instructions:

1. Warm the water (not boiling, just comfortably warm).
2. Add fresh lemon juice and olive oil to the water and stir.
3. Drink immediately, preferably on an empty stomach in the morning for maximum benefits.
4. Optional: Add a pinch of sea salt to help balance electrolytes.

Nutrition & Benefits (per serving):

- Calories: ~25
- Antioxidants: **High**
- Detoxification: ✓
- Digestion Support: ✓
- Hydration: ✓
- Liver Support: ✓

MEDITERRANEAN DIET COOKBOOK FOR SENIORS

Welcome to a journey that will transform the way you eat—one flavorful, wholesome meal at a time. This 28-day plan brings the vibrant tastes and proven health benefits of the Mediterranean diet to your table with simple, satisfying recipes designed especially for seniors.

More than just a meal plan, this is your roadmap to eating well without stress or complicated rules. Whether you're cooking for one or sharing meals with loved ones, these recipes will help you enjoy the Mediterranean lifestyle—where good food, good health, and good company come together naturally.

Let's begin your 28-day adventure in delicious, nourishing eating!

Day 1

Breakfast: Apple-Cinnamon Chia Pudding (Prepped the Night Before)
Lunch: Grilled Eggplant & Chickpea Wrap
Dinner: Roasted Chicken Drumsticks with Garlic & Paprika
Snack: Spiced Roasted Chickpeas
Dessert: Lemon Semolina Cups (Lightened Up)
Beverage: Warm Lemon Water with Olive Oil

Day 2

Breakfast: Spinach & Feta Egg Scramble
Lunch: Mediterranean Turkey Burger
Dinner: Stuffed Zucchini Boats with Turkey & Feta
Snack: Zucchini Fritters with Yogurt Dip
Dessert: Orange & Almond Flour Cookies
Beverage: Cherry-Pomegranate Smoothie

Day 3

Breakfast: Almond Butter & Banana Toast with Chia Seeds
Lunch: Sardine & Avocado Toast
Dinner: Seared Tuna with White Bean Salad
Snack: Ricotta-Stuffed Cherry Tomatoes
Dessert: Tahini Bliss Balls with Dates & Sesame Seeds
Beverage: Fig & Almond Smoothie

Day 4

Breakfast: Warm Quinoa Breakfast Bowl with Almond Milk & Berries
Lunch: Roasted Red Pepper & Hummus Wrap
Dinner: Quinoa-Stuffed Tomatoes with Basil & Goat Cheese
Snack: Hard-Boiled Eggs with Olive Tapenade
Dessert: Chia Pudding with Almond Milk & Figs
Beverage: Orange-Date Smoothie with Tahini

Day 5

Breakfast: Cucumber, Hummus & Smoked Salmon Wrap
Lunch: Chicken Souvlaki Skewers with Tzatziki
Dinner: One-Pan Mediterranean Chicken & Veggies
Snack: Roasted Red Pepper Hummus
Dessert: Ricotta with Berries & Balsamic Glaze
Beverage: Mint & Green Tea Infusion

Day 6

Breakfast: Mediterranean Smoothie with Spinach, Banana & Olive Oil
Lunch: Mediterranean Tuna-Stuffed Avocados
Dinner: Lentil & Sweet Potato Stew
Snack: Marinated Olives with Orange Zest
Dessert: Baked Medjool Dates Stuffed with Almond Butter
Beverage: Mint & Green Tea Infusion

BONUS: 28-DAY MEAL PLAN

Day 7

Breakfast: Mediterranean Smoothie with Spinach, Banana & Olive Oil
Lunch: Vegetable & Feta Stuffed Pita
Dinner: Baked Tilapia with Herbed Quinoa
Snack: Zucchini Fritters with Yogurt Dip
Dessert: Olive Oil Citrus Cake (Naturally Sweetened)
Beverage: Mint & Green Tea Infusion

Day 8

Breakfast: Spinach & Feta Egg Scramble
Lunch: Stuffed Bell Peppers with Quinoa & Feta
Dinner: Salmon with Lemon-Dill Yogurt Sauce
Snack: Marinated Olives with Orange Zest
Dessert: Cardamom-Spiced Apricot Compote
Beverage: Zucchini & Pineapple Smoothie

Day 9

Breakfast: Almond Butter & Banana Toast with Chia Seeds
Lunch: Zucchini Noodles with Pesto & Cherry Tomatoes
Dinner: Stuffed Zucchini Boats with Turkey & Feta
Snack: Stuffed Grape Leaves (Dolmas)
Dessert: Mini Greek Yogurt Cheesecakes (No-Bake)
Beverage: Olive Leaf Tea with Lemon

Day 10

Breakfast: Greek Yogurt with Honey, Walnuts & Fresh Berries
Lunch: Tuna & White Bean Salad
Dinner: Vegetarian Moussaka
Snack: Hummus with Veggie Sticks
Dessert: Cardamom-Spiced Apricot Compote
Beverage: Chamomile & Lemon Balm Tea

Day 11

Breakfast: Zucchini & Herb Omelette with Goat Cheese
Lunch: Stuffed Bell Peppers with Quinoa & Feta
Dinner: Zucchini Noodle Stir-Fry with Tofu
Snack: Hard-Boiled Eggs with Olive Tapenade
Dessert: Couscous Pudding with Almond Milk & Orange Blossom
Beverage: Cherry-Pomegranate Smoothie

Day 12

Breakfast: Whole Grain Pita with Hummus, Sliced Egg & Cucumber
Lunch: Greek Chickpea Stew
Dinner: Spinach & Feta Stuffed Chicken Breast
Snack: Baba Ghanoush with Seed Crackers
Dessert: Cinnamon-Stewed Plums with Greek Yogurt
Beverage: Spinach, Banana & Olive Oil Smoothie

Day 13

Breakfast: Ricotta & Fig Toast with Walnuts
Lunch: Roasted Cauliflower & Lentil Bowl
Dinner: Grilled Sea Bass with Olive Tapenade
Snack: Tomato Bruschetta on Whole Grain Toast
Dessert: Coconut Date Rolls
Beverage: Pear & Ginger Smoothie

Day 14

Breakfast: Greek Yogurt with Honey, Walnuts & Fresh Berries
Lunch: Baked Cod with Tomato & Olive Tapenade
Dinner: Mediterranean Vegetable Casserole
Snack: Mini Caprese Skewers
Dessert: Rosewater Pistachio Bites
Beverage: Fennel & Licorice Root Tea

Day 15

Breakfast: Tomato, Basil & Mozzarella Breakfast Sandwich
Lunch: Chickpea & Spinach Patties
Dinner: Lemon Herb Baked Chicken Thighs
Snack: Cucumber & Feta Bites
Dessert: Greek Yogurt with Honey & Walnuts
Beverage: Avocado-Cucumber Mint Smoothie

Day 16

Breakfast: Red Pepper & Goat Cheese Breakfast Wrap
Lunch: Spinach & Olive Whole Grain Pasta
Dinner: Cauliflower & Chickpea Tagine
Snack: Mini Spinach & Feta Phyllo Triangles
Dessert: Spiced Poached Apples in Herbal Tea
Beverage: Cucumber-Lemon Detox Water

Day 17

Breakfast: Mediterranean Cottage Cheese Bowl
Lunch: Grilled Chicken Shawarma Bowl
Dinner: Baked Eggplant Parmesan (Lightened Up)
Snack: Warm Herbed Olives & Almonds
Dessert: Ricotta with Berries & Balsamic Glaze
Beverage: Coconut-Yogurt Smoothie with Pistachios

Day 18

Breakfast: Herbed Tomato & Egg Skillet
Lunch: Shrimp & Orzo Salad
Dinner: White Fish en Papillote with Lemon & Herbs
Snack: Mini Falafel Balls with Tahini Sauce
Dessert: Baked Pears with Cinnamon & Walnuts
Beverage: Carrot, Orange & Ginger Juice

Day 19

Breakfast: Savory Avocado Toast with Cherry Tomatoes & Olive Oil
Lunch: Caprese Quinoa Bowl
Dinner: Shrimp Saganaki with Tomatoes & Feta
Snack: Mini Bell Peppers Stuffed with Hummus
Dessert: Fig & Almond Energy Bites
Beverage: Sage & Rosemary Herbal Tea

Day 20

Breakfast: Mediterranean Oats with Almonds, Dates & Cinnamon
Lunch: Lentil & Feta-Stuffed Sweet Potatoes
Dinner: Grilled Lamb Chops with Rosemary & Garlic
Snack: Lentil & Herb Salad Cups
Dessert: Lemon Yogurt Mousse with Olive Oil
Beverage: Watermelon-Basil Smoothie

Day 21

Breakfast: Apricot & Walnut Greek Yogurt Bowl
Lunch: Eggplant & Tomato Stew (Caponata Style)
Dinner: Chard & Cannellini Bean Sauté
Snack: Greek Yogurt & Herb Dip with Crackers
Dessert: Pasteli (Greek Sesame-Honey Bars – Small Batch)
Beverage: Mint & Green Tea Infusion

Day 22

Breakfast: Chickpea Breakfast Hash with Bell Peppers & Onions
Lunch: Herbed Chicken Pita Pocket
Dinner: Grilled Sea Bass with Olive Tapenade
Snack: Stuffed Grape Leaves (Dolmas)
Dessert: Couscous Pudding with Almond Milk & Orange Blossom
Beverage: Celery, Apple & Parsley Juice

BONUS: 28-DAY MEAL PLAN

Day 23

Breakfast: Zucchini & Herb Omelette with Goat Cheese
Lunch: Bulgur Salad with Parsley & Pomegranate
Dinner: Eggplant & Lentil Ragu over Whole Wheat Pasta
Snack: Mini Caprese Skewers
Dessert: Olive Oil Citrus Cake (Naturally Sweetened)
Beverage: Cherry-Pomegranate Smoothie

Day 24

Breakfast: Peach & Yogurt Parfait with Pistachios and Mint
Lunch: Mediterranean Lentil Salad
Dinner: Vegetarian Moussaka
Snack: Hard-Boiled Eggs with Olive Tapenade
Dessert: Chia Pudding with Almond Milk & Figs
Beverage: Coconut-Yogurt Smoothie with Pistachios

Day 25

Breakfast: Poached Eggs with Sauteed Kale & Garlic
Lunch: Shrimp & Orzo Salad
Dinner: Grilled Lamb Chops with Rosemary & Garlic
Snack: Smoked Salmon on Cucumber Rounds
Dessert: Cardamom-Spiced Apricot Compote
Beverage: Orange-Date Smoothie with Tahini

Day 26

Breakfast: Ricotta & Fig Toast with Walnuts
Lunch: Grilled Chicken Shawarma Bowl
Dinner: White Fish en Papillote with Lemon & Herbs
Snack: Lentil & Herb Salad Cups
Dessert: Baked Pears with Cinnamon & Walnuts
Beverage: Chamomile & Lemon Balm Tea

Day 27

Breakfast: Tomato, Basil & Mozzarella Breakfast Sandwich
Lunch: Roasted Red Pepper & Hummus Wrap
Dinner: Greek Lemon Chicken Soup (Avgolemono)
Snack: Hummus with Veggie Sticks
Dessert: Lemon Semolina Cups (Lightened Up)
Beverage: Watermelon-Basil Smoothie

Day 28

Breakfast: Red Pepper & Goat Cheese Breakfast Wrap
Lunch: Chickpea & Spinach Patties
Dinner: Spinach & Feta Stuffed Chicken Breast
Snack: Spiced Roasted Chickpeas
Dessert: Orange & Almond Flour Cookies
Beverage: Fennel & Licorice Root Tea

A FINAL TOAST TO MEDITERRANEAN LIVING

As we close this culinary journey, remember: the Mediterranean diet isn't just about what's on your plate—it's about reclaiming the joy of eating while nourishing your best self. For seniors, this timeless approach offers more than protection against chronic diseases; it delivers a recipe for vibrant living where every meal becomes an opportunity to celebrate health, connection, and life's simple pleasures.

Picture this:

Your kitchen transformed with a few thoughtful tools—a steady cutting board, a comfortable knife—turning meal prep from chore to cherished ritual. Mornings beginning with a fluffy omelet packed with herbs and veggies, ready in minutes yet fueling hours of vitality. Afternoons brightened by crunchy vegetables with lemon-tahini dip, proving healthy snacks can be both convenient and crave-worthy. Evenings gathered around a table where good food and laughter flow as freely as the olive oil dressing your seasonal salad.

This is the Mediterranean promise—a lifestyle where:

- Food is medicine that delights your senses while protecting your heart and mind
- Cooking is creative yet effortlessly simple
- Every bite connects you—to tradition, to loved ones, to the earth's natural rhythms

Let these pages be your compass toward lasting well-being. May your Mediterranean journey be seasoned with discovery, shared stories, and the quiet satisfaction of caring for yourself as thoughtfully as you've cared for others. Here's to your health—may it be as rich and vibrant as a sun-ripened tomato, as enduring as an ancient olive tree, and as joyful as a shared meal under open skies.

Bon appétit and buona vita!

REFERENCES

REFERENCES

Altomare, R., Cacciabaudo, F., Damiano, G., Palumbo, V. D., Giordano, M. C., Bellavia, M., Tomasello, G., & Lo Monte, A. I. (2013). The Mediterranean diet: A history of health. *Iranian Journal of Public Health, 42*(5), 449–457. https://www.ncbi.nlm.nih.gov/pmc/articles/PMC3684452/

Capurso, A. (2024, March 23). *The Mediterranean diet: a historical perspective.* Aging Clinical and Experimental Research; Springer Science+Business Media. https://doi.org/10.1007/s40520-023-02686-3

Cleveland Clinic. (2022). *Mediterranean Diet.* Cleveland Clinic; Cleveland Clinic. https://my.clevelandclinic.org/health/articles/16037-mediterranean-diet

Doctor's Desk. (2023, July 21). *Revolutionize Your Weight Loss Journey: Embracing the 10 Best and Smart Diet Plans for 2025.* Clinikally. https://www.clinikally.com/blogs/news/revolutionize-your-weight-loss-journey-the-10-best-and-smart-diet-plans?srsltid=AfmBOoqgtbBBX1n24j8wuVwhU6Zy-wX51qnEt3aHi9w2Dltj8jQp1aV6

Elder-Friendly Kitchen Essentials for Easy Meal Prep. (2024, March 9). Pro Chef Kitchen Tools. https://prochefkitchentools.com/blogs/tips/elderfriendly_kitchen_essentials_for_easy_meal_prep

Kim, J. Y. (2020, October 27). *Optimal diet strategies for weight loss and weight loss maintenance.* Journal of Obesity & Metabolic Syndrome. https://doi.org/10.7570/jomes20065

Mayo Clinic Staff. (2021, July 23). *Mediterranean diet: A heart-healthy eating plan.* Mayo Clinic. https://www.mayoclinic.org/healthy-lifestyle/nutrition-and-healthy-eating/in-depth/mediterranean-diet/art-20047801

Ros, E., Martínez-González, M. A., Estruch, R., Salas-Salvadó, J., Fitó, M., Martínez, J. A., & Corella, D. (2014, May 1). *Mediterranean Diet and Cardiovascular Health: Teachings of the PREDIMED Study.* Advances in Nutrition. https://doi.org/10.3945/an.113.005389

Simplify Meal Prep: Top Cooking Assists for Elderly Individuals. (2024). Rosariumhealth.com. https://www.rosariumhealth.com/blog/top-cooking-assist-for-elderly

Widmer, R. J., Flammer, A. J., Lerman, L. O., & Lerman, A. (2015, March). *The Mediterranean Diet, its Components, and Cardiovascular Disease.* The American Journal of Medicine. https://doi.org/10.1016/j.amjmed.2014.10.014

Printed in Dunstable, United Kingdom